SKETCHES OF A
BIBLE ILLUSTRATOR

SKETCHES OF A BIBLE ILLUSTRATOR

TRANSLATING SPIRITUAL TRUTH
INTO VISUAL FORM

LOUISE BASS

BASS POND
TRAVERSE CITY, MI

Published by
Bass Pond
PO Box 3131
Traverse City, MI 49685
basspondbook@gmail.com

Publisher's Cataloging-in-Publication Data
Bass, Louise.

    Sketches of a Bible illustrator : translating spiritual truth into visual form / Louise Bass. – Traverse City, MI : Bass Pond, 2013.

    p. ; cm.

    ISBN13: 978-0-9860384-0-2

    1. Bass, Louise. 2. Women missionaries—Papua New Guinea—Biography. 3. Missions—Papua New Guinea. I. Title.

BV3680.N52 B37 2013
266.009953—dc23   2013934946

Project coordination by Jenkins Group, Inc.
www.BookPublishing.com

Cover painting and interior illustrations by Louise Bass
Layout design by Yvonne Fetig Roehler

Printed in the United States of America
17   16   15   14   13 • 5   4   3   2   1

Thank you Ann Wilkinson,
you are the editor I prayed for.

You advised, taught, corrected, encouraged and
prayed for me as I gathered my life's story
into meaningful words.
May the Holy Spirit continue
to empower and use you.

CONTENTS

TROPIC HAZE

My thoughts tumbled over each other like coffee beans on a conveyer belt as I began to regain consciousness. Overhead, a whirring fan created yellow and orange swirling designs on a tiled ceiling. Abstract waterscapes were framed in a row of windows like a hazy blue ocean—or was it the sky? I fought in vain to focus on the disheveled puzzle pieces. People moved, floated, stared at me. I thought, *Am I dreaming? Where am I?*

Snail-like, the pieces slowly came together. White sheets covered me up to my neck. Bars guarding my feet became the foot of a bed—a hospital bed! The ocean was the tropical Pacific. I assumed I was near the Pacific Ocean and in a hospital bed. "How did I get here?" I wondered. Fear gripped me. "Where are Jack and the children? What happened? If only I could remember."

Through the fog I saw an efficient-looking uniformed nurse coming toward my bed, and I chose my words carefully. I asked, "Can you tell me what day it is, where I am, and how I got here?"

"You are in the Wewak Government Hospital on the New Guinea coast, dear, and today is July 18, 1962," she answered in a soothing Australian accent. "You were brought here in a Catholic mission jeep from the airstrip."

I sputtered, "Please ... tell me ... why ... I'm here."

"You'll need to ask the doctor when he comes," she said, dismissing my question on her way out of the room.

I felt strange and wondered whether I would ever feel normal again. Then, slowly I started to recall. I knew I worked as a missionary with the Wosera-speaking tribe in New Guinea. I lived in a tiny village near the wandering, crocodile-inhabited Sepik River with my husband, Jack, and our two children, Jonathan and Joye. Jack and I were Wycliffe missionaries trained as translators for this group of people who had no written language. While I was trying to clear my mind, a proficient-looking Australian doctor came and stood at the foot of my bed.

"G'day," he said. "Glad to see you're awake. How do you feel?"

"Well, I don't know. I feel strange, detached, and I can't seem to think coherently or remember correctly. How did I get here? Where are my husband and children?"

The doctor's white starched coat rustled as he took a worn clipboard from the bottom of my white hospital bed.

"Looks like you collapsed in the Wosera village," he said. "Your husband made radio contact with the hospital, and we got in touch with the nearest mission plane service and requested a coastal airlift for you. Your family is staying here in Wewak until you recover. Then we'll talk about your return to your mission headquarters in the highlands. However, we definitely don't want you going back to the Wosera village."

Oh, no, I thought. *Not return? That can't be true. That's my calling! Our goal! I can't believe a loving God would allow us to receive linguistic training and jungle survival skills, give us the dream of translating the Bible into an unwritten language, and then let us fail. Oh, Jesus, don't let this happen! Enable me to be strong and continue the work we started nearly a year ago for the Wosera people.*

Just then, a volunteer aide in a uniform and pink apron walked into my room. She was pushing a wooden book cart, and I immediately fantasized about her coming to my bed and whispering, "My dear, I suffered with the same symptoms you have, and now I'm completely well. Don't be alarmed."

Encouraged, I dozed off. When I awoke, Jack and the children stood by my bed. Four-year-old Jonathan and two-year-old Joye, both buttoned into multicolored woolen sweaters selected by their dad (who never felt the tropical heat as I did), peeked at their pale mommy in the white sheets. I was delighted to see them, but their little faces clouded over with concern when they saw their mother so incapacitated. After a bewildering visit with Mom, the children eagerly left the room and scurried down the hall to the more comfortable world outside. Jack kissed me good-bye.

Good-bye? Good-bye? Am I dying? What's wrong? Why doesn't the doctor tell me something? I wondered in desperation.

Questions raced through my worried mind. My latest symptom was an atypical numbness starting in my feet and traveling up to my waist. I was afraid that when this absence of feeling reached my heart, I would be a goner. Yes, I knew I belonged to God, but I desired to stay and serve him.

A torrent of questions invaded my apprehensive mind. *Why would a caring God take me away from my precious children? Why would a loving God allow me to be cut down in this way? Why would we be prevented from continuing our important translation work? How would my illness affect our relationship with our new friends among the Wosera clan?*

I worried. I tossed. I prayed. The 12-hour days and 12-hour nights of the equatorial time zone passed lazily in the warm confines of the hospital room. Jack, Jonathan, and little Joye were lodged in a mission guesthouse and visited me when possible. Nearby, a sandy beach offered a playing place for the children and a reading spot for their dad.

Wanting to do something meaningful and creative, I asked the humorless nurse whether she could get me some embroidery floss, a needle, scissors, and a dispensable pillowcase. Using the materials she brought me, I penciled in Isaiah 26:3 from a King James Bible found in my bedside cabinet: "Thou wilt keep him in perfect peace whose mind is stayed on thee." The violet and green chain-stitched letters crookedly followed the hem of the white case and, with my pillow inside it, gave me reassuring comfort while God's Word gave me much-needed hope.

My husband also gave me hope. He never complained about the disappointing problems I unwittingly caused him by my weakness and inability to concentrate on the work we came to do—learning the language. Instead, he earnestly prayed for me and for whatever changes loomed in the unforeseen future. His faith in a loving God was amazingly enduring.

One morning, Jack surprised me. Carrying a tennis ball, he strode into my room with the children in tow. At home, a brisk game of tennis often relaxed him after a day of intense biblical studies at his desk. *Did he expect me to play tennis in my weakened condition?* No, instead he positioned us to play four-cornered catch. Little Joye loved chasing the ball under the beds or chairs, and Jonathan tried hard to catch it. Unfortunately, the game ended when the paralyzing feeling again crept into my feet and then took all sensation from my legs and lower body. These strange symptoms I had kept from Jack, but now I desperately cried, "My feet—I can't feel anything, and the numbness is moving upward. What should I do?"

Jack calmed my disturbing panic by saying, "It's OK. Just react to this symptom as you would a headache. It comes, it moves, and finally it leaves."

His reassuring words quickly relieved my unreasonable fear of dying. That night I slept well and dreamed about the doctor. When he came in to check on me, he asked how I slept.

"Very well, thanks," I replied. "I dreamed about you and the nurse."

The next day they discharged me with a small bottle of tranquilizers and the order *not* to return to the Wosera village. *Do they think I'm a mental case?* The thought of going back to the Ukarumpa center, and not to the village, caused me embarrassment. Surely, our inability to return to the village would disappoint our director, our supporting churches, the Wosera people, and all our missionary friends. Again, we were at a crossroad of decision. What did God have in mind for us? We thought we followed his guidance. We prayed. We prepared. We promised. Where was he leading us now?

Making plans to fly from Wewak on the coast back to Ukarumpa in the Eastern Highlands seemed painful, but with heavy hearts we contacted the Wycliffe aviation department by two-way radio and learned that one of our mission planes could pick us up in Wewak in two days. The guesthouse facilities were still available, so we settled in to wait for the flight. Jonathan and Joye enjoyed being near the water, while Jack and I struggled to make sense of this unexpected setback. We had arrived in New Guinea in 1960 planning to translate the Bible for a group of people without a written language, and now we were leaving those people—only two years later.

While we waited in Wewak, I reminisced a great deal about our past. My memories went back to the very beginnings of our life story and continued up to the present bewildering situation.

1

CUT OUT FOR ART

Pierre of France

In September 1935, my only sister, Audrey, entered kindergarten in a Detroit, Michigan, school near our home. I followed her the next year. The teacher, Mrs. Tower, played piano, taught us simple ditties, and assembled us into a musical band. Wearing little blue capes and hats, we sat in green painted Goldilocks chairs on the school lawn and entertained passers-by. The really lucky kids got to play small instruments and real drums. Shyly, I received a metal stick and triangle to strike a "ping" at the right moment. I played my part, but I secretly coveted the more important instruments like the kazoo and oatmeal box drums.

My mother, before her marriage, taught in a one-room schoolhouse in Ontario, and my dad studied electrical engineering in Detroit. Drawing and sketching played a part in both my parents' careers. They influenced me, and before I was six years old, I learned to draw a simple brick house. A front view with a central door, windows, and a porch with steps completed the drawing and my architectural repertoire. This artistic talent went largely undiscovered at school until the approach of Christmas created a need for a cardboard fireplace and chimney for Santa's arrival in the spacious kindergarten room. The teacher questioned whether anyone in the class could draw bricks. My hand shot up, and the job fell to me.

I drew with some skill and painted timidly until the red brick fireplace became a reality to behold. I became the *class artist,* and I was called upon to create activity posters, simple greeting cards, and 3-D dioramas constructed in shoe boxes. My shy delight in expressing myself through artwork was fueled with compliments and attention. My artistic talent, prompted by my mother's instruction, awakened within me the gratification that accompanies appreciated personal expression.

Being educated in the standard American system was the norm for most of my school years, except for one life-changing difference. On the opening day of my junior year in high school, my mother escorted me via bus to downtown Detroit to enroll me in the fashion illustration course at Cass Technical High School. My mother couldn't have known this would be the most excellent education I could have for my future work or that, someday I would be drawing ethnic people wearing their unique garments in far-away places.

Our Christian parents took my sister and me to church regularly, and we both believed and trusted in Jesus when we were young teenagers. Audrey loved to sing and later attended Detroit Bible Institute (now Tyndale College). I decided after meeting missionaries from Africa that I wanted to use my talent to do artwork in Sudan, Africa.

After graduating from Cass Tech, I was asked by my caring pastor, "Well, Louise, what do you plan to do with your life now?"

"I want to be a missionary and artist in Africa," I answered.

He thought for a moment and then seriously replied, "There are a lot more important things for you to do in missions than artwork!"

He was innocently mistaken, of course, but his remark brought puzzlement and discouragement and led me down several blind alleys before I could get back on the track God prepared for me. I believed God had a purpose for me; how to discover it became my assignment.

Occasionally, in Detroit, a Christian chalk artist presented a youth program, and I watched in awe. To witness a gifted artist rapidly attack a large paper-covered board on an easel and cleverly wield just the right colored chalk to create a powerful God-centered visual message for an entire church congregation intrigued and fascinated me. To observe an orange-streaked sky, backlit lavender clouds, sap-green foliage, and multicolored figures appearing on the board, captivated my imagination. While soft recorded music played in the background, my eyes, like those of the viewers around me, were ecstatically riveted as the artist secretly switched on and gradually brightened the ultraviolet light from behind the board. Then, like magic, a central figure would come into sight in the glowing majesty of brilliant color. It aroused gasps and wonder from the amazed audience. God's power, utilizing art, reached the hearts of many viewers.

At the conclusion, a pastor often addressed the congregation and added meaning and biblical references to the theme of the drawing. Furthermore, he would effectively emphasize and encourage biblical guidance for our lives. My heart was touched! Desire awoke. I wanted to do this! I would learn how to reach people for Jesus Christ using this powerful visual communiqué. My goal became more focused after graduating from college and landing a job in a commercial art studio.

Enthusiastically motivated, I located a portable upright drawing board, assorted chalks, and a teacher to show me the basics. I began to draw for congregations in local churches. As my repertoire increased, I always prayed about which scene God would want me to use to profit the needs of the audience. Some folks found the drawings worshipful, some enlightening, and some life changing.

Then one Sunday morning, from my vantage point in our Baptist church choir loft, I noticed a young man in a khaki uniform with sergeant's stripes on his sleeve. His family attended the church, and he visited after being honorably discharged from the army. Gossip among the single women stressed his availability, but they were not attracted to his desire to work overseas. It sounded appealing to me.

I discovered that Jack (John) Bass was the sixth of eight children born to a Greek immigrant father and a German mother. Living in inner-city Detroit, the family gravitated to the City Rescue Mission, where most of them became believers in Jesus Christ at the evangelistic meetings. Jack excelled in high school and made his family proud by earning a scholarship to study medicine at the University of Michigan. He finished his pre-med courses and then decided to leave the university and serve his country in the Korean War. His older brother, Gust, died in Normandy in World War II, and his three other loyal brothers took up arms. Jack's patriotism led him to enlist in the U.S. Army as a medic. It was 1951.

During Jack's military service, a dedicated Christian chaplain befriended him in Germany. Jack's commitment to Jesus grew stronger. After two years in the army, he enrolled in the Detroit Bible Institute with a goal to minister overseas. After church one Sunday evening, he asked if he could drive me home. That led to our attending church functions together. My love and respect for Jack and his strong commitment to Jesus Christ grew, and I knew I wanted to spend the rest of my life with this faithful man.

2

CHARTING THE
COURSE

Snowflakes danced in the wind on January 21, 1956, as Jack and I pledged undying love to each other at the front of our decorated church filled with happy family and friends. My sister, Audrey, the matron of honor, forgot my ring in her purse, so I made my vows while wearing our nervous pastor's wedding ring. In the church basement, trays of homemade goodies were offered to the hungry guests as Mr. and Mrs. Jack Bass were later chauffeured away in the backseat of a 1955 red Chevy.

After a honeymoon in Pennsylvania, we moved into an upstairs apartment on Detroit's east side. Jack drove to the Bible College daily, and I rode the bus to a commercial art studio where I helped create Dodge Export advertising. Supper in our modest kitchen became our planning time. We both were confident that God wanted us to be in some kind of mission work, and we began gathering information about various organizations. Jack had a friend who worked with Wycliffe Bible Translators (WBT) learning an unwritten language in Alaska.

"Alaska ... maybe we should go there," we considered.

We sent for WBT literature, and their brochure listed personnel needs. Two categories caught our attention, visual artists and language scholars. We responded.

On account of the skills WBT needed, they required all applicants to attend SIL, the Summer Institute of Linguistics at the University of Oklahoma in Norman. The course would not interfere with Jack finishing his BA degree in the winter; consequently, we attended SIL that summer for the linguistic training.

Oklahoma in summer heated up like an oven. I was pregnant. Sensitivities to smells and tastes assaulted my growing body. Sitting in stifling classrooms, I experienced nausea stimulated by the strong scent of newly mown grass outside the open classroom window. However, I managed to survive the smells, the discomfort, and the heat. We finished the required WBT linguistic requirements and aced the course! It was time to head home to Detroit.

On February 5, 1959, a 10-pound baby boy was delivered to us in Detroit's Women's Hospital. Nurses saw his crib labeled "Bass" and joked about him singing bass in the "Hallelujah" chorus. The next summer we returned to Oklahoma with our precious baby, Jonathan. Somehow, by God's grace, we managed to care for him, study between his feedings, and pass the tough academic course plus meet all the requirements for approval to attend Jungle Camp

This survival training camp was located in southern Mexico. I must admit I had motherly reservations about taking our infant son to a steaming jungle. Would he be strong enough for the hostile environment? What about snakes, malaria, river rapids, insects? Jack and I discussed the risks. We prayed about the dangers. We counted the cost of our commitment. Yes, we agreed, the assignment's dangers were uncertain and the hazards unknown, but we knew the Lord, our Shepherd, had prepared us for whatever challenges might lie ahead. Our baby boy was in God's hands. We were all going south of the border!

Our parents shed tears but swallowed their fears and prayed for our safety. Jonathan, a husky, healthy 10-month-old infant, traveled happily as long as he held on to his favorite blanket. Jack drove while I read the maps taking us from Michigan to Mexico. We eagerly anticipated the adventure ahead of us.

After meeting with our mission contacts in Mexico City and leaving our car, we traveled by bus over precipitous mountain roads to the semitropical state of Chiapas near the Guatemala border and entered new territory. For the last few miles, I held Jonathan as we rode in on a burro. The training camp appeared in a jungle clearing near a rapidly flowing river.

We entered the small center where a number of grass-roofed huts provided shelter. About 30 campers from the United States and Canada, including singles, couples, and small families, arrived, supervised by 12 skilled friendly staff members. Two young mothers and I each carried our little ones in long hand-woven *rebozos* draped across our shoulders. Babies were bathed in hand-hewn wooden tubs. Hiking, swimming, building, learning, and eating all brought us together like a large family, and after a month at the main base, we were ready for the more isolated survival phase of our training.

Jack and I were directed to a spot in the jungle where we put our new and untried skills to work. I built a playpen/crib from rattan cane growing nearby to keep our crawling baby safe. Jack built a sheltering lean-to, a double bed, and a clay oven, where I cooked oatmeal and even baked a pineapple upside-down cake. Our instructors kept a *bodega* storehouse where we could collect fresh rations each day.

Once settled, we practiced survival techniques, centered on a plane crash scenario. The men had to leave their wives and children and spend a night alone in the jungle while using their food-finding and shelter-building skills. After their adventure, the men returned, and we women left our children with their dads and took our turn at surviving.

Baby Jonathan cooed and squealed along with the jungle sounds of birds, cicadas, and frogs while safely zipped inside his bug-proof army-surplus hammock. When we hiked in the surrounding hills, Jonathan went along in his daddy's backpack.

On February 5, 1960, Jonathan turned one year old, and we celebrated with tacos, peanut butter, and lemonade, while Jonathan was satisfied with powdered milk and a banana. Our jungle training nearly over, we put up our hammocks in trees near a landing strip and waited overnight for the missionary plane to come and take us out. We survived survival training! Now officially Wycliffe Bible translators, we could enthusiastically sing a verse from *Amazing Grace,* "Through many dangers, toils and snares, we have already come; 'Tis grace has brought us safe this far, and grace will lead us home."

What next? More and more, Jack and I felt drawn to investigate missionary work in New Guinea. This island country in the South Pacific lay just north of Australia and became a protectorate under Australian rule following World War II. Furthermore, at that time only missionaries from commonwealth countries could apply to enter New Guinea. Strangely, Jack and I knew that was where God wanted us to work in his kingdom. By the time we managed all the preparations for missionary work—acquiring sufficient promised financing, accumulating basic household goods, applying for and obtaining passports, and purchasing passage—the ban was lifted. Coincidence? Hardly! God opened the door. This lifted ban gave confirmation to our souls' yearnings. Our investigations had not been in vain.

In several months we boarded the HMS *Orcades* in San Francisco. She was an old British passenger ship, and we literally sailed into our new life! We disembarked in metropolitan Sydney, Australia, after two long weeks on the water. Jack carried Jonathan and I shouldered the diaper bag as we said "Cheerio" to the ship, gathered our ample baggage, checked into a Sydney mission guesthouse, and settled down for a three-week wait while our crate of household necessities traveled by slow boat to New Guinea. Also waiting at the guesthouse was another family of Wycliffe missionaries, Al and Dellene Stucky and their young son, Mark, who became Jonathan's playmate.

We celebrated Jonathan's second birthday in the no-nonsense accommodations of the guesthouse

He had a considerable appetite. No one could expect such a young child to understand that the milk and bread supply was limited. From his highchair, with childish impatience, he very loudly demanded, "Bea! Bea!" We understood "bread," but to the Aussie guests, as their raised eyebrows hinted, it sounded like "Beer, Beer!" I believe the host and hostess were relieved to see us leave.

From Sydney, with the Stuckys, we flew north in a commercial plane over the Bass Straits to our port of entry, Port Moresby, the capital city of the island of New Guinea. Jack and I were eager to get to our destination after the long wait in Sydney and relieved to meet the pilot, who introduced us to an ancient DC-3 cargo plane. He strapped both families onto the wooden benches lining the sides of the cavernous interior. What an experience! No large windows allowing sightseeing but the bumpy flight and ear pressure assured us we were gaining altitude. When we landed, the old plane lumbered along a sloping dirt runway and shuddered to a stop. Shaken but excited, we deplaned.

The welcoming committee at Kainantu village arrived scantily clad; most were wearing sarongs (*laplaps* in Pidgin English), a few wore T-shirts and some were adorned with feathers or flowers. Many bare-foot dark-skinned people with gleaming white smiles encircled us as soon as our well-shod feet hit the red earth. A smile is a welcome in any language. Our hearts were warmed as we exchanged this international greeting. White men they knew, white women they had seen, but a couple of two-year-old white "pickaninnys" they greeted like rock stars!

After a month and a half of travel, we finally stood on New Guinea soil, where God led us! Gradually, the sea of people parted, and two WWII open jeeps edged toward us. Waving enthusiastically, our new director called out, "You made it! Welcome to the Territory of New Guinea!"

With a smile and a greeting, the Stuckys got into one jeep, and I climbed into the open back of the other. Jack handed Jonathan to me and then slid into the front seat to get acquainted with the director, Jim Dean. My thoughts swirled like the haze of ocher dust as we bumped over nine rutted miles. I didn't feel fearful. Close to my husband and child, I felt secure. But one small detail scared me. From somewhere in the grassy hills I heard jungle drums beating. That ominous rhythmic sound brought up unwanted images of "savages" firing up an enormous pot for "missionary stew."

Are Jack and I, and especially little Jonathan, safe here? I fretted. Then, holding Jonathan a bit tighter and with the road getting bumpier and bumpier, I leaned forward and yelled to Jim, "What's all the drumming about?"

"Oh, the drumming—that's just workers at the government agricultural station making music on their break," he called over his shoulder. "They're harmless," he added, sensing my apprehension.

I had a lot to learn.

3

LINGUISTS AT LAST

Because of the isolation and inaccessibility of New Guinea, its geography and culture acquired the label "Stone Age." It became known that deep in the unexplored mountains, tribes practiced cannibalism. However, following World War II, in the 1950s and '60s, things rapidly changed. Largely as a result of the arrival of international "outsiders," the culture was gradually transformed. World-renowned scientists traveled to the South Pacific to study undocumented birds, plants, and diseases. Anthropologists were intrigued to discover a pristine treasure trove of customs, languages, and kinships. Australian patrol officers established roads, airstrips, agricultural stations, and government centers such as the town of Kainantu. As a result, some of the inhabitants of New Guinea were beginning to acquire Western cultural traits, practices, and trading skills.

Back, in 1934, American missionary Cameron Townsend sold Spanish Bibles in Central America and realized that the Indian people needed to have access to the Bible in their own languages. He founded the Wycliffe Bible Translators organization to train linguists in the methods of Bible translation for languages around the world. In 1950, the island of New Guinea possessed at least 750 spoken languages that had never been written—a linguist's gold mine.

Wycliffe sent the first Australian missionary linguists into New Guinea in 1955. It wasn't long before other young missionaries trained in linguistics began to arrive on the island. Jack and I arrived in 1960, and by then a tract of land in the Eastern Highlands had already been obtained for a language center called Ukarumpa (pronounced "ookarumpa") after a local village. Initially, indigenous groups were contacted using New Guinea Pidgin spoken by the missionaries and others to determine whether the people wanted their language to be written. They did.

New Guinea advanced rapidly as coffee, tea, and other local cash crops flourished and were exported to an expanding commercial world system. Island economics and evangelism were copartners in the discovery and development of written languages for the fascinating peoples of New Guinea. No longer were they stigmatized with the Stone Age label.

A whirlwind of the "new and different" describes our first year at Ukarumpa. Our New Guinea lessons included living in a woven rattan cane house with bamboo floors, carrying buckets of water up from the nearby river, buying sweet potatoes at the open-air market, wondering when the rainy season would end, potty-training Jonathan in the out-house, and getting to know our dedicated coworkers. We were allotted a swampy section of grassland that only needed drainage ditches and we had an ideal spot for our home to be built. The profession of carpenter did not appear on Jack's résumé, so he secured the help of several newly arrived friends, including Phil Staalsen and Al Stucky, to put up the framework. Built up on three-foot local pine posts, the house would survive the tropical rains and occasional earth-tremors. Other materials such as louver windows, cement siding, wooden doors, and plywood sheets arrived by trucks from the coastal town of Lae. Our Ukarumpa home was taking shape. I hoped they would finish quickly because our second child's arrival was fast approaching.

Our initial plans to work in New Guinea did not include living permanently at Ukarumpa. When the house neared completion, Jack flew to the distant Sepik River area to explore possibilities and places where we might work. He settled on a small village on a grassy plain where the tribal people spoke Wosera. Eager for us to come live with them, these kind tribal people offered to build us a temporary house from jungle materials where we could stay while learning the language. It would include a shed for Jack's study and an outhouse. Jack brought all this news back to me, and we prayed for God's blessing on our new venture with the Wosera tribe in the Sepik Province.

In the meantime, our unfinished Ukarumpa home at the center needed more work, so we temporarily shared another missionary's home. My pregnancy progressed without problems. We arranged to have a mission plane fly us to the Lutheran hospital in Madang on Monday, August 7, 1961, near my due date. The Sunday morning before we planned to fly out, we awoke in the windowless room to get ready for church. I also planned to prepare a meal for a coworker we had invited for lunch after worship. Suddenly, I felt the twinge of labor pains. Attending church was out of the question! Things began moving quickly. There would be no dinner guest on that Sunday or scheduled flight on Monday. Jack ran to the meeting-house to find an Australian nurse, and she quickly arrived with her friend—both were trained midwives. When they saw the dark bedroom, they immediately found someone with a vehicle who drove me to another more suitable birthing house.

Eight miles away in Kainantu, a government doctor managed a small clinic. One of the colleagues drove there and enlisted his services. Fortunately, he arrived at Ukarumpa only minutes before Joye Louise arrived. Through all this, my concerned and somewhat pale husband stood ready by my bed to help. The midwife nurses monitored my breathing, and with a couple of pushes, Joye entered the world. Her name suited her from the start.

With grateful, happy hearts and much relief, Jack and I thanked God for this precious gift of new life. Of course, there were no weight scales, but we could clearly see that our new daughter was more petite than her big brother, Jonathan, had been at birth. She had lovely brown hair and brown eyes. Her rosy cheeks were rare on fair-skinned children conceived in a tropical climate.

Time passed quickly. Our home at Ukarumpa was finally finished. We moved in with our few belongings. Jonathan, now three, played in the morning with children in the small preschool run by coworkers. We found love and togetherness as a new family, in a new home, in a new country.

When Joye reached six months, we packed up our home and flew to the Wosera village to begin our language studies. We settled into the specially built village house. The sago leaf roof kept the rain out and invited the geckos in. Our beds were draped with netting to discourage mosquitoes. The raised floor was made of black palm wood, and there were open spaces between the boards—it made sweeping the floor a breeze! Finally, we reached our place of service eager to do God's work.

Before long I realized that successfully fitting into a preliterate culture, as the anthropologist Margaret Mead skillfully achieved, seemed impossible to Louise Bass. I tried, but I was often culturally challenged. When the "sorcerers" danced into the village with the rushing sound of dried grass capes and frightful masks, my success at adapting to the culture was strained. I earnestly tried to convince my terrified little Jonathan, who was hiding under the bed, that these scary-looking beings were harmless people—just costumed men. Later, however, when I inquired about this custom, I learned that the actual purpose of the witch doctors' visit was to frighten the children!

While visiting with some local women at the half door in Jack's office, I discovered that they were curious about how I fed baby Joye. Since breast milk was the best and only milk available, I nursed her for a year and a half, but my modesty when breast-feeding meant covering up this private process. However, the native women thought nothing of hurrying through the tropical village in the buff! I thought about our orientation-class instructions. We were encouraged to appreciate and embrace the unusual customs of others.

Consequently, when Joye's feeding time arrived, I called the women, in a language of combined Pidgin and Wosera, to come to the door. Then, throwing my reserve to the wind, I let the women peek under Joye's concealing blanket. In spite of my inability to understand their exclamations, I believe they were saying, "Oh, yes, she is a woman! She has breasts. She feeds her baby like we do!" I guessed I successfully jumped that cultural hurdle. Margaret Mead would have been proud of me! I also think that incident with the women proved to be a kind of bonding experience for us all.

One afternoon, two preteen girls came to the half door while chewing on something. Part of me didn't want to know, but they came specifically to show me what they ate for snacks. One girl opened her hand to reveal a tarantula-like spider with brown furry legs that had been toasted in the fire. She yanked off each leg separately and tossed it into her mouth. My orientation lessons vanished again as my hands flew up to my face in horror. "Oh, Lord, help me out of this one!" Controlling my emotions, I tried to make up for my rudeness with a feeble smile. Actually, I should have felt right at home with those big "harmless" spiders. Whenever I went to the rough-hewn outhouse at night, my flashlight reflected the glowing red eyes of such spiders hidden in between the slats of sago branch walls—ever-present company! I never felt the desire to partake of that Wosera snack.

On a Saturday two weeks later, we traveled north about 20 miles on the dirt road in our old army jeep. We drove past the Maprik Governmental Center, a medical clinic and a nearby experimental agricultural station where skilled Australians researched various cash crops such as peanuts, coffee, and tea. We were on our way to visit with Australian friends John and Ruth Burgin. When Jack first went to explore the area, he met this Christian family with their two preteen children. They lived and worked in agriculture near Maprik. The Burgins became our dear friends, our important mentors, and our essential contacts with the outside world.

Once, Ruth came to our village and lovingly planted flowers around the foundation posts of our simple home. She helped us obtain bananas, sweet potatoes, papayas, greens, flour, and eggs, all of which were not available at the local trade store. Whenever we visited the Burgins, we were encouraged and inspired. John entertained us with his infectious sense of humor and local stories, while Ruth had the knack of preparing gourmet meals from the limited foods available. Having these friends within driving distance helped us maintain our purpose, goals, and well-being.

Our children's activities in the Wosera village were varied and adventurous. Jonathan often played with some of the village children but cautiously stayed close to home. When his daddy got an urgent request to transport a sick or injured neighbor to the Maprik medical clinic, three-year-old Jonathan climbed up into the jeep very close to him and became part of the mercy missions. The open back of the jeep filled up with the patient's concerned kinfolk. Emotions ran high on these trips, and Jonathan's stories of clinic rides entertained us.

On sweltering afternoons, I took Joye and Jonathan to the narrow, cool river west of the village where the women did laundry. We splashed in the refreshing water safely separated by miles from the crocodiles basking on logs in the dangerous Sepik River. Life was different on the mission-field for families and their children, but our shared adventures created good memories and tight bonds of family unity.

As a busy wife and mother, I observed many of the native customs. Jack, on the other hand, could usually be found in his outdoor study pursuing accurate meanings of the language in order to correctly translate Bible passages into Wosera. He often worked with a likeable young local man named Gabriel. Jack would ask questions, jot notes, decipher language codes, and practice his language skills. Then, with the children safely tucked in for the night, Jack and I would walk into the village center and join the locals sitting around a bonfire. Here we would try out our newly learned words and phrases. Once I innocently embarrassed the group and myself when I unknowingly said the colloquial word for "female sexual organ." Oops! I made a mental note not to say that again.

Jack and I learned much about native beliefs around those evening campfires. For instance, twinkling fireflies flashing around us were believed to be spirits of the dead returning to haunt relatives whose wailing and grieving were inadequate. Another custom regarding death involved burying the dead person in a deep grave with a length of hollow bamboo protruding from the top. That allowed the escape of flies hatched on the corpse. The direction of the flies was carefully observed because they led the kinfolk of the dead person toward the village of the sorcerer who caused the death. Then there was a "payback" as sorcery was worked on the "guilty" party in the other village.

Our hope was to help break this cycle of sorcery and death when we could tell of God's love in their language. How long would it take for us to learn enough of this culture and customs to produce a Wosera Bible to be understood in this strange land? We were certain that God wanted us to share his truths with these people. He would help us understand and deliver.

Five months dragged by in the jungle heat, then six, then seven. It was 1962. It was hot and humid, and I became very weighed down. I felt oppressed in the tropical climate and became lethargic, listless, and languid. The very thought of working on the language or assisting Jack with a reading class exhausted me. My energy as mother, missionary, wife, artist, homemaker, and friend of the locals turned into weariness and passivity. My zeal was escaping like air out of a balloon. Fatigue followed me. Apathy attacked me. Was the stifling heat the cause? Was I demanding too much from myself? Where was God's promised strength? Were two active children too much for me? Or was this lassitude a physical malady? A greater fear arose in my heart. Was I becoming mentally unbalanced?

Eventually, the day came when I completely collapsed onto the bed in our temporary home in Wosera. The young woman who helped me in the house ran outside to get Jack. Since I was unable to move, Jack loaded me into the jeep and then drove the whole family seven miles to a Catholic mission where I was transferred to their single-engine plane and flown to Wewak on the Pacific Coast and to the government hospital, about a 20-minute flight.

***

Back in the foreword of this book, I told the story of that bewildering hospital experience. After the hospital discharge, we waited for the plane to take us home. That doctor had been unsure of my malady and issued me tranquilizers. Because of my lethargy, I decided that the last thing I needed was to be more tranquil, and threw away the bottle of pills, for better or worse. Soon we would leave Wewak and go home to Ukarumpa.

4

BACK TO BASICS

At last, our mission Cessna arrived at the Wewak airstrip to take us away from the Wosera village forever. Jim, our pilot greeted us with a smile and a "howdy." He stowed our belongings and language materials in the Cessna's cargo pod and said, "We should have a smooth flight back to Ukarumpa. By the way, I heard about your illness, Louise, and I wondered if you would like to see the Baptist doctor for another opinion. She works in a mission hospital in a remote mountainous area that's right on the flight plan. I can radio her and then land on the hospital airstrip. We will still make it back to Ukarumpa in time for supper."

I looked at Jack. He nodded in agreement with the plan, so we climbed up into the two-seater. Jack and Jonathan got into the back-seat, and I held little Joye in front. Jim checked the fuel gauge and shut all the doors for takeoff. Silently, we said good-bye to all we left behind. After a bumpy start, the flight was quite smooth. Joye went to sleep, and three-year-old Jonathan pressed his nose to the window to look down on the jungle of treetops. Soon, the small plane touched ground on a high inclined airstrip and taxied to a red-dirt clearing.

The doctor, an attractive middle-aged woman, stood back until we climbed out of the plane and then greeted each of us warmly. Jack and the children sat in the shade and watched the pilot as he talked to the local people who gathered to check out the plane. The doctor directed me up a steep path cut in the tall grass that led to the mission com-pound. After inviting me into her antiquated office, we sat down and she began to ask questions. I tried to adequately describe my symptoms, but it reminded me of trying to split a coconut with a dull machete. She nodded and seemed to grasp my attempts. As she settled back in her chair, I began to feel more comfortable.

In layman's language, she told me that each person has a fragile component. It is the way God created us. Therefore, he knows our indi-vidual vulnerable makeup, whether physical or psychological. When we undergo unendurable stress, the chink in our armor causes a breakdown in that area.

"For example," she explained, "if a missionary with weak lungs contracts TB under extreme stress, forcing him to return to his homeland, his constituency may honor him as a godly hero who gave his all. However, the exhausted missionary who succumbs to a psychological weakness may be considered a failure by his supporters and himself."

She continued, "I work to combat this misunderstanding. Sometimes primitive living conditions and escalating temperatures strain newcomers. Heat may well be your unavoidable culprit. I suggest you go back to the cooler altitude and work in predictable surroundings for a few months and see whether your health returns. Let me know how you're doing. May God bless you and your family."

I hugged and thanked her. Outside, Jack held baby Joye on his shoulders and clasped Jonathan's small hand in his, waiting patiently for me to join them on the downhill hike back to the airstrip. The pilot and his single-engine Cessna were also waiting for me. Catching up, I slipped my arm around Jack's waist.

"Wow! I don't think I lost my mind after all. What a God-send she is," I said to him.

Tramping down the trail, I relayed the doctor's words to Jack. We walked past bush huts, long grasses, and colorful wild birds. Thanks to the lifting of my emotional burden, all the colors seemed shades brighter.

With the five of us belted into the plane, we careened along the rough runway, teetered, and quickly gained altitude. In the backseat, tired Joye relaxed into sleep on her daddy's lap. Jonathan was just tall enough to join Jack and gaze out at the thick, impenetrable rain forest below where snow-white sulfur-crested cockatoo parrots perched in the massive jungle treetops. When the friendly pilot offered to let me take the controls, I shook my head and laughed, saying I needed visible landmarks. Fortunately, he and his instruments kept us moving eastward for the 45-minute flight. With the welcome dose of confidence the doctor spooned out to me, I felt ready to look the future in the eye—whatever it might hold.

We put down on the Aiyura airstrip and spotted a well-worn van waiting for us near the garage-sized airplane hanger. With our baggage tossed in the rear, we took our seats and headed home. Breathing in the cool, refreshing 5,000-foot air, we set out for Ukarumpa and the familiar surroundings of the home we had left. I secretly pondered whether I would ever again be able to live in stifling tropical heat.

Home at last! We left our cozy metal-roofed home with expectations of living in a grass-roofed, bamboo-walled house for at least a year to assimilate as much of the language as we could. Now, in fewer than six months, we were back where we started from with heavy hearts. We felt our vision and goal slipping away, as my strength had done. In short order, we unpacked and settled into our Ukarumpa home, with an unseen, unassigned future.

I couldn't help but wonder, *What would my friends think of me now? Why wasn't I the strong, pioneering missionary I set out to be? Were my motives less than pure?* I thought my motive was to serve God, so why did I care what people thought? I felt ashamed of my weakness and questioned whether in grasping onto the dream of being a Bible translator I had put my wish to succeed above my desire to serve God as he wanted me to, in his way.

I knew that God, in his mercy, knew all about our situation, and I committed my insecurities to him, once again. Although I believed the doctor's theory, the "how" and "why" questions didn't stop surfacing in my mind. Believing the Bible as the source of truth and life was central to our lives, and we longed to make this truth available to these Bible-less people. We desired God's plan for eternal life to be placed in their hands for them to read for themselves. I pressed on day by day with hope while clinging to Philippians 1:6: "Being confident of this, that he who began a good work in you will carry it on to completion until the day of Christ Jesus."

My husband's unfaltering reassurance and faith became great sources of support for me. Jack met with our translation director, who recognized and acknowledged Jack's biblical knowledge. Now, assigned as a consultant for other missionaries needing help in understanding and translating difficult biblical passages, my husband was blessed by God. My heart was encouraged. Our gracious God knew we needed to have our faith fortified at this precise moment in time. Working diligently at his job, playing hard on the tennis court, or consistently helping me with the children, Jack was a leading example to me of flexibility, determination, and loyalty. He certainly handled our "failure" better than I did.

At this time we were anticipating the birth of our third child and our director strongly advised us to fly out early to the Madang Lutheran hospital in case of unforeseen complications. We arrived in plenty of time. However, I waited in lonely isolation at the almost-vacant hospital while my anxious husband helped Joye and Jonathan pull through chicken pox in a mission guesthouse.

On August 8, 1964, baby Jackie needed some help with her arrival, and we were grateful for the experienced doctor who skillfully assisted with her safe delivery. With lovely reddish-blond hair and blue eyes, her fair coloring was opposite that of her brown-eyed brother and sister. We all loved her and knew she was one of us. Our family was complete.

My thoughts went out to other Christian wives. I wished I could tell them, "Ladies, if you think you cannot survive, cook, give birth, and raise a family in a foreign land, think again! Pray earnestly about your calling! Don't think you can't! You can with God's help!"

While stateside, more than once, a woman came to me with tears in her eyes while she told me that her husband was trained and called to work overseas but she feared raising a family out of their homeland and, consequently, they stayed home—unfulfilled. Grandparents also need to seek God's wisdom regarding "letting go" of their children and grandchildren. Most mission organizations that accept families maintain competent and considerate care of parents and children.

Our family loved introducing our newly arrived and delightful Jackie to our colleagues at Ukarumpa and to local friends. In the mornings, Jonathan and Joye were cared for in a well-run preschool. When I learned that my morning assignment awaited me in the Wycliffe print shop at Ukarumpa, I devised a plan to keep my precious baby Jackie right next to me. I borrowed a baby carriage from a British missionary couple living nearby and wheeled Jackie to work with me daily. She snuggled, napped, and played immediately adjacent to my work space. My heart rested as I easily fed and ministered to my daughter's needs and the printer's needs. It was God's gift.

At the well-equipped print shop, I rendered black-and-white drawings for the short, inexpensive reading books of vernacular stories used by translators such as Ed and Aretta Loving. The Lovings hiked while carrying their two young daughters, often for days, into the New Guinea Mountains to live with the Awa people and learn their unwritten language. With a goal of giving them a readable New Testament, the Lovings called together the nearly naked men and bare-breasted women to a scenic outdoor "chairless classroom." They sat on tree stumps or empty kerosene cans and looked at the booklets, sometimes upside down, amazed that their talk could be put on paper. In the print shop, I drew simple black ink illustrations of arrows, possums, bananas, and so on, to be printed onto alphabet charts or slim booklets enabling nonreaders to understand the written words.

I had grieved the loss of that kind of one-on-one involvement with the local people, but the joy of creating literacy materials for even more people lit up my heart like the bright morning sun rising above a dark, silhouetted mountain.

5

NEW PLANS

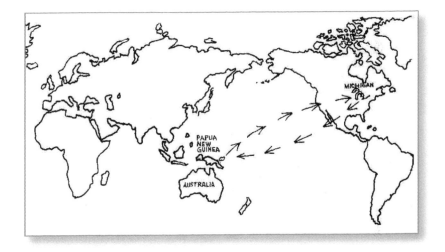

After our first five years in New Guinea ended in 1965, the time had come for us to travel back to America for a one-year furlough. It would be difficult to walk away from our friends and coworkers at Ukarumpa, but spending time with our aging parents in Michigan was important. Jonathan was six, Joye four and a half, and Jackie 18 months. We would be introducing them to their eager grandparents. Priorities included acquainting our children with other relatives, eating American food, and, of course, connecting with our supporting churches. A newly assigned family of translators would live in our Ukarumpa home, so we stored away the things we didn't need, in order to temporarily make room in our home for a new family.

Jack and I walked hand in hand across the bumpy dirt road to say good-bye to our neighbors Dennis and Nancy Cochrane. Unexpectedly, Dennis told us about his health problems. He was plagued by weakness and exhaustion, and he anticipated receiving help from a circulation specialist in Philadelphia when they got back to the United States. My antenna went up. Perhaps this expert could help me also. We'd been praying and asking God for my complete return to health. Could this be an answer to our prayers?

We decided it was. Jack agreed we should see this doctor in Philadelphia, and within a few busy hours, he revised our plane tickets to make a stop in the "City of Brotherly Love." Tickets, passports, diapers, and toys in hand, we reached our destination, weary but hopeful. A Philadelphia taxi conveyed the five of us through the overwhelming city to the circulation clinic. Jet-lagged, Jack sat in the chair-lined waiting room and held a wiggly Jackie while a speechless Jonathan and a wide-eyed Joye sat on either side of him. Sending up a quick prayer for their patience, I followed a friendly nurse to the consultation room.

Dr. Frederick Erdman, in his 60s, wore black-rimmed glasses, and his fingers intertwined over his ample chest. He listened to my list of erratic symptoms. I answered his questions. Instantly, he grasped my problem and explained it as follows:

"The symptoms and experiences you have had indicate that you have a lack of arterial tone in your circulatory system. A number of missionaries who have lost their health because of the oppressive tropical heat, which causes diminishing arterial tone, have been able to overcome this ailment. Not only have they recovered but also they have been able to remain in the tropics, continuing their work for years. It is not a psychological matter; it is thoroughly physical. However, the subject has received little attention from most doctors."

The treatment he prescribed called for cool spinal applications whenever the symptoms appeared. It was as simple as dipping a Q-tip in cool rubbing alcohol and running it along my spine! He left me alone in the examining room to get a book for me to take with us. I considered my situation. This cure seemed too simple, too incredible. How could something so uninvolved and uncomplicated remedy the debilitation I suffered? "Cool therapy" to alleviate my loss of energy? A Q-tip and alcohol used to remove my extreme fatigue?

My mind wrestled with my spirit. I pondered the past, the prayers, and the hopes Jack and I had shared. Then I remembered that I had been specifically directed to this place, to this doctor. No matter how strange or unusual, I was determined to give Dr. Erdman's prescription a try. After all, I reasoned, didn't Jesus use spit and mud to heal a blind man? If this worked, I could go into the oppressive heat and know how to control my "arterial tone" even if I needed to stand under a cold-water bucket shower.

As I was leaving, Dr. Erdman gave me some last advice that sounded as implausible as his prescription: "If you're going to live in that godforsaken place, you need to take a vacation off the island halfway through your next five-year stay."

I laughed to myself because we had no discretionary money to buy expensive plane tickets to Australia or anywhere else. Besides, God had not forsaken either New Guinea or us. I applied the treatment as needed and was able to continue to serve in New Guinea. Praise God!

Leaving Philadelphia, we continued on our interrupted journey to Detroit and happy reunions with grandparents, families, and friends. We mapped out the year ahead in Michigan. Renting a house in a quiet neighborhood provided a nearby school for six-year-old Jonathan and four-and-a-half-year-old Joye. Excellent teachers, new friends, and street crossing guards helped the children adapt to strange new American culture. Jackie played contentedly at home while Jack and I sorted our photo slides, planned meetings, and spoke in churches on weekends. Jack also was eager to attend a Healing Prayer Conference.

In New Guinea, ailing coworkers occasionally called on Jack to pray for them. Our friend Marey Todd, suffering with asthma attacks approached Jack and asked him to pray for her. He set up a time to meet with Marey and her husband, Ralph, and he prayed for healing from her debilitating bouts. Later, Marey contacted Jack to express her gratitude that she had been free of the asthma attacks for months. "Could this be a spiritual gift of healing?" Jack wondered.

His teaching about spiritual gifts was limited, and he desired to learn more from someone with experience. He didn't know much about the speaker, Francis McNutt, but had read one of his books and wanted to hear more of his experiences of praying for the sick. We left the children with their delighted grandparents and drove to a Bible camp near Lake Michigan, where the conference was assembled.

In our first group session, we were asked to stand, introduce ourselves, and reveal our expectations and reasons for attending. Muffled by my hand, I whispered to Jack, "I don't know what to say. Please speak for both of us." He rose and gave a brief account of our translation work in New Guinea, his experience in seeing people healed, and his desire to know more details of healing prayer. Next, a middle-aged man stood and identified himself as a minister of a large church in Chicago; he was also interested in prayer for the sick. From beside him, his rather pale wife stood and said, "My name is Gail, and I had surgery to remove a threatening brain tumor. God graciously healed me; I'm here to thank God for his healing in my life." She sat down.

Afterward, Jack walked me to the women's rustic sleeping cabin, kissed me good night, and departed for the men's dorm. A top bunk was assigned to me in a nearly full women's dormitory, and Gail lay on the bottom bunk below me. Soon after "lights out," the bunk bed began to tremble. Alarmed and concerned, I lay very still wondering what to do.

I concluded that Gail must be experiencing unbearable pain. My thoughts darted: *was she suffering from some other condition? She testified to a miraculous healing. What's going on? Was this my chance to pray, even though I knew nothing about critically ill people? What would Jack do?* Because he seemed to have that spiritual gift, I knew he would pray and ask God to heal Gail. I knew that 1 Corinthians 12:7-10 lists healing with other gifts of wisdom, knowledge, faith, miraculous powers, prophecy, distinguishing between spirits, tongues, and the interpretation of tongues. *But I had no spiritual gifts—or did I? How could I know?* Maybe God's Holy Spirit was waiting for me to put him to the test. The only way I'd discover what to do was to act.

Fearfully, I pushed myself to the edge of the thin mattress and literally dropped to the cold cement floor. I leaned forward until my face was close enough to hers to be heard and whispered, "Gail, are you OK?"

"No," she managed, "I'm having the same pain I had with the tumor. I don't know what's happening to me. God help me! Could you assist me to the bathroom?"

"All right," I replied quietly, not wanting to wake the other sleeping women. With Gail holding tightly to my arm, I helped her to the bathroom, where I switched on a light, guided her in, left her, and waited. "What do I do now?" I silently worried. Before long, she opened the door and teetered forward, clutching my arm. However, we didn't make it back to her bed. Gail collapsed on the closest empty bottom bunk. I knelt beside her to pray and as soon as I tried to pray, I sensed pain invading my body, similar to flu symptoms. My head ached. I felt nauseated. I was weak. I could not pray.

Suddenly, a strip of yellow light appeared from a nearby door that slowly opened, revealing a silhouette of a tall woman.

Oh, good, I thought, *God is sending an angel to pray for Gail.*

The visitor rudely snapped, "What's wrong with her?"

No, she's no angel, I deduced, but I uttered weakly, "It's Gail; she's in unbearable pain and believes her tumor has returned."

"No," the woman retorted, "that's impossible. Gail had surgery and was healed. That's why she came here."

"She needs help," I blurted out. "Please pray for me. Gail's pain is evidently severe, and for some reason I'm feeling it also."

Then this brusque woman who refused to pray for the "healed" woman said an abrupt prayer for me and, mysteriously, my pain left— and so did the stranger. She disappeared through the doorway and returned shortly with Gail's preacher husband. He rushed in, bundled his shuddering wife into their vehicle, and left to make the difficult drive home to Chicago.

Clambering up into my bed, I slept restlessly until the morning gong announced breakfast. After breakfast, I shared all these puzzling events with my husband to ponder. The conference finished. The time arrived to start our trip home.

After being away from family for three days, we eagerly rejoined our well-cared-for children. Eight days later, an envelope arrived containing the dreaded announcement of Gail's funeral. That unexpected news left me grief stricken. I was thoroughly confused. No more wondering whether the Holy Spirit had given me a spiritual gift of healing. If I prayed for people to be healed and they died, I wanted no part of it. Another personal failure filled me with unanswered questions. I was emotionally confused for days. Jack was not put off; his prayer ministry grew; he was steady and sure. I was perplexed.

Prolonged farewells, careful packing, and the busyness of moving turned our thoughts to going "home" to New Guinea. We took time to purchase and pack a chalk drawing board, lights, chalks, and paper to ship ahead. Each of us had benefited from our year with loved ones. We left with heartfelt emotions and promised to return to the United States in five or six years.

This time, we were a family of five traveling by train to California, visiting friends, and boarding the HMS *Orcades* again to take us back to New Guinea. The children enjoyed on-deck activities and swimming in the pool. Docking in Hawaii, Fiji, and New Zealand gave us opportunities to explore other unique cultures and scenic Pacific islands. Our stay in Australia was shorter than the first time. There were friends to visit in Sydney before flying north to New Guinea's capital, Port Moresby. From there, we flew up into the Highlands and landed at Ukarumpa, our home sweet home. Our one-year furlough had been a success because we were helped by Dr Erdman. With his suggestions we knew we could return to Papua New Guinea. Jack benefited from our time at the healing seminar and we all enjoyed being with our loved ones in America.

6

UKARUMPA AND
BEYOND

We returned to New Guinea in 1967, rested and ready to buckle down to our Wycliffe assignment for the next five years. Jonathan and Joye traveled daily on the antique double-decker bus with their "mates" to the primary school across the bridged river. Jackie went to the mission preschool in the mornings. Jack conscientiously consulted with translators to assure accuracy in the scriptural texts.

In the print shop, I continued creating illustrations for literacy books. Free time found me in the rustic art studio that Jack built for me overlooking our backyard—an enticing forest of green eucalyptus trees sloped down to a rushing river. To paint portraits of New Guineans in their multicolored feathered headdresses became my desire, but acrylic paints dried too fast to blend the subtle flesh tints. Sitting in my studio and pondering my problem, I heard a clear but inner voice say, *Try oils!* It was so authentic I remember it as God's voice. In spite of my awe, I wondered, *Where on this island could I find tubes of oil paint?* The answer came: a friend going on furlough asked whether I would accept the gift of his oil paints! I felt like I had been "anointed with oil."

My paintings became more refined, the portraits more realistic. One headdress painting was purchased and given to the American ambassador. Although that gift helped cement Wycliffe's diplomatic relationships, I did not neglect my print shop assignments. Soon, government people, tourists, and missionaries purchased nearly everything I painted. The pounds and shillings I received were set aside to pay for our next furlough travel to America. It was Gods loving provision.

Five days a week, Jack sat at the table in the translation center. Missionaries came in from their villages and brought their language helpers and their questions for consultations. He came to grips with scripture: the good, the difficult, and the misunderstood. He had solid biblical training, but like a ghost in the closet, the Holy Spirit and his gifts were unavailable resources for both of us. Our biblical education was conservative and "accurate," but the Holy Spirit's work described in the New Testament was relegated to another dispensation. My interest in the

Trinity—Father, Son, and Holy Spirit—remained vague and reserved. Assigning the Spirit to other church denominations or groups, I quietly dismissed it from my agenda. My focus was family and work. With acknowledgment to God for physical healing and returned strength, I thought my fulfillment was complete.

Jack, on the other hand, during his in-depth sessions with his fellow translators, examined Bible verses such as those Paul wrote to the church at Corinth in 1 Corinthians 12:7: "Now to each one the manifestation of the Spirit is given for the common good." Jack could not avoid the many scriptural references to the Holy Spirit. How could translators express these truths in another language unless they understood them themselves? How could Jack help the translators make sense of these scriptures unless he believed and lived them? How could some Christians say they believe in the Trinity and neglect the third person? The more Jack studied about the significance of the Holy Spirit, the more God revealed his truth to him. But he didn't share much of this enlightenment with me because I wasn't interested.

Something new was happening at Ukarumpa. An enthusiastic gathering of our fellow workers began meeting on Saturday evenings to sing praises to God and share biblical teaching. Jack loved it, and I tagged along. He sang ardently; I sang indifferently. Jack closed his eyes and raised his hands in gratitude; I closed my eyes and hoped nobody noticed me. Chairs arranged in a circle left no place to hide. I clutched tightly to my Bible and my doubts.

My thoughts ran like this: *Why did Jack wander so far from his traditional Bible college education? This teaching about the Holy Spirit appeals to those who are needy. I'm not needy. I was sick and weak, and now I am well and strong. I don't need anything but my faith in Jesus Christ. Maybe we're both ready for a break. If the Holy Spirit empowers us to do God's work, why doesn't he send us money for a restful vacation off the island?* I judged irreverently. I hadn't forgotten the Philadelphia doctor's advice. My faith wavered hot and cold inside me; little did I know the richness our Father God waited to lavish on us.

The answer to my questioning came in the form of a newspaper article from Port Moresby. Large letters announced, "South Pacific Games to be held on the island of Tahiti." A contest sponsored by Tang, the orange drink, promised a Tahitian holiday to the winner of a random drawing. With high hopes and nothing to lose, I mailed my contest entry. After waiting for two weeks, I received word that I had won the trip! Excitement, shock, and thankfulness to God swept over me. Even the children joined in the thrill because they would get to stay in the Ukarumpa children's home with their friends.

We arranged for the children to be taken care of and then made the trip to Port Moresby. We flew from New Guinea to Brisbane, Australia, and on to New Zealand and, finally, the French island of Tahiti. We were pampered, entertained, fed, and blessed by the friendly people who greeted us. Attending soccer games, tennis matches, races, and other sporting events brought refreshment to our minds and bodies. We even checked the church situation to see whether a Bible translation was needed, but the book was already available in French and Tahitian. After two awesome weeks, we reluctantly packed our bags, left the island, and headed home.

Seated on the jet, flying home over the ocean, we pondered our luxurious vacation. My thoughts turned to prayer. *Lord, I love you, and I know you loved me first. I don't deserve your love. Forgive me for all the times I've let you down. Forgive my weak faith in you. You have blessed us over and over, and now you've given us this amazing adventure. Your Word is true. You promised to supply all our needs according to your glorious riches in Christ Jesus. You know our future. You know our strengths and weaknesses. Thank you for giving me a godly husband. Thank you for giving us three precious children to enjoy and bring them up to know you. I praise you, Father, Son, and Holy Spirit. My heart is overflowing.*

Two weeks from the day we left, Jack and I climbed out of the mission Cessna at the Aiyura/Ukarumpa airstrip. Our reunion with the children included hugs, kisses, and breathless stories of their adventures. They were sick with measles during our absence; however, they all looked healthy and happy at our homecoming. We were ready to be together as a family again.

Life returned to normal. Jack and I continued our work, and the children carried on with their schooling. The calendar showed Easter coming soon. Many of the missionaries came from their villages to Ukarumpa to spend the holidays with their children. Local New Guineans and language helpers also came. Easter provided an opportunity to gather in the meeting house to hear inspirational speakers and special musical numbers and also provided the perfect occasion for a chalk drawing.

I was asked to provide the visual depiction of the Easter story. First I chose a pianist to supply appropriate music. Then, I decided to draw as though the viewers were inside the dark interior of the empty burial tomb looking out over the garden at first light. Beyond the open entrance of rolled-away rocks, several kneeling women wept. In the center of the garden stood the unseen figure of the resurrected Jesus that I had drawn ahead in special "invisible" chalk. At the end of the presentation and using the ultraviolet light, I gradually brought a brilliantly lit Jesus figure into the viewers' vision. The room remained breathless for a sacred moment. Suddenly, audible gasps and cries of wonder exploded! Exclamations of delight erupted from the amazed New Guineans and missionaries alike. God had used this visual means to speak to hearts!

Finally, the overhead lights lit up the meeting room and the music ceased. Jack and I began to dismantle the chalkboard and put away the chalks. Small groups of curious people lingered around the front benches and talked among themselves. Then, Mary Stringer, an Australian translator, came toward us with two middle-aged men from the Waffa language group. They had not only heard but also read the crucifixion story because Mary and her partner translated the Gospel of Mark into their language and taught them to read. Yet, prior to this evening, they could not believe Jesus actually awoke from death, arose from the grave, and was resurrected. Tonight, after seeing the drawing, the truth of the biblical account dawned on them, and they became believers! Such joy!

Several months later, Mary told us the great news that these men were now leaders in their fledgling village church and had led other Waffa people to believe the truth of the gospel story: Jesus Christ died on the cross for our sins, arose from the dead, ascended into heaven, and sent his Holy Spirit to teach, guide, and empower us.

Looking back over the past five years, Jack and I were reminded of the river that ran behind our house. Coming down from the mountains, it grew wider, with small rivulets joining the journey toward the ocean. As the river wound around to form the boundary of our Ukarumpa community, it made a change in its course. The course of translation we started on also made a turn, but we continued to flow toward the same goal—to give God's Word to Bible-less people.

Educationally, this had been a good five years for our children. Caring teachers came as volunteers from other English-speaking countries. Each year the pupils chose projects for a science fair, such as growing rare orchids or displaying unusual insects and butterflies. Our girls learned to crochet, sew, and play the piano. Jonathan conquered driving, first in a soapbox car, then on a motorbike, and, finally, in our Volkswagen Beetle. He also learned to be careful of the pigs that freely roaming the dirt roads and were most precious to their owners. By the time of our second furlough, we had to consider the implications for our children's education.

Because of the extra cash I earned by selling paintings, we were able to chart a family rail trip through Europe in 1972. We packed our bags, rented out the house, and settled our family into five seats on a jet to Athens, Greece, and a map to adventure. Jonathan, Joye, and Jackie learned about their ancient Greek heritage while walking around the Acropolis and Parthenon. We met Jack's Greek-speaking family members in Corinth, and they took us into their homes and hearts.

On the Greek coast of the Adriatic Sea, we boarded the Brindisi ferry to Italy and then the northbound train. We toured Venice, Rome, and Florence, where the Uffizi Gallery provided my first encounter with an original oil masterpiece. As I stood before *The Birth of Venus* by Botticelli, tears of wonder flowed down my cheeks. I also wept through art galleries in Rome and Paris while Jack entertained our offspring in parks and zoos. We visited Darmstadt, Germany, where Jack had been stationed, and paid a visit to the Evangelical Sisterhood of Mary.

In Austria, the children enjoyed the tour of the underground salt mines and also the zoo, where we saw some rare animals from New Guinea. Our European vacation completed, we made our way to Luxemburg and then on to our final destination, Detroit, Michigan.

After a five-year absence, we were faced with many questions. American relatives and friends eagerly inquired, "It's so good to have you home; where will you live?" "Where'll the children attend school?" "What do you plan to do this year?" Little by little, the answers materialized with God's grace guiding us. The former parsonage of our home church served as our temporary home, and gracious carpooling enabled all three children to attend a Christian school. Speaking and showing slides of the New Guinea work filled our weekends. The year rushed by, and soon we were in the skies again, heading for New Guinea, grateful to our Heavenly Father for the needed furlough but eager to return to our calling and the desire of our hearts.

7

A GLORIOUS GIFT
GIVEN

Could it be 13 years since we first arrived in Ukarumpa? Jack's consulting skills, sharpened on the grit of experience, smoothed many a translator's journey from original biblical text to meaningful words in tribal languages. My art job—putting spiritual truth into visual form—aided the understanding of printed words in many languages as translators added my ink drawings to their writing. Together, we knew the joy and satisfaction of being part of God's plan and love for the world.

Still, I dug my heels in regarding the work of the Holy Spirit. Slowly, I began to question my preconceptions—oh, not enough to admit I had a spiritual need but enough to wonder what I was missing. Yes, missing! Did I, the woman with no needs, say that?

The Saturday night praise meeting continued to draw an interested group of missionaries, including Jack and me. In spite of our center's location, off the speakers' circuit, inspirational speakers from Australia, America, and England were invited to New Guinea, and they came to give us Bible-based teaching. Dr. Alan Redpath, a British evangelist, pastor, and author from Moody Church in Chicago, traveled to Ukarumpa in 1975 to speak to the Wycliffe people at the Easter Bible conference from the prophecy of Ezekiel in chapter 47 of the Old Testament. He painted a word picture of the river flowing out from God's temple, portraying the Holy Spirit. With measured, imaginary footsteps, we walked into the stream and went forward until it became a river of water to swim in. Yes, brush stroke by brush stroke on the canvas of our minds, Dr. Redpath pictured a scene revealed to those with eyes to see and ears to hear—a spiritual vision presented in spoken form.

The second-generation missionaries, our children, profited from the speakers and the praise music. Jackie Ruth, the 16-year-old daughter of Jack and Chick Ruth, added her zeal to her classmates' with her enthusiastic singing, as their choir sang "I Want to Tell the World about Jesus." With her vibrant personality and exceptional leadership abilities, we all knew Jackie was headed for great things.

Our small home-fellowship group met Friday evenings. On Good Friday 1975, about 10 of us gathered at Ralph and Marey Todd's for prayer and communion. A ringing phone broke our quiet fellowship. As our host, Ralph, held the phone to his ear, we waited. He listened, turned slowly, and broke the silence with crushing news: "Jackie Ruth has gone to be with the Lord in a motorcycle accident."

We were struck speechless—silenced. No! Oh, God, not Jackie. "Be with her parents right now," someone prayed. More silence. We tried to grasp this devastating news. How could this be true? Jackie was part of our Ukarumpa family. She had so much potential. She was loved. Now the Lord had taken her home? Most of us were too stunned to cry. We shared our grief, hugged good night, and silently walked back to our homes.

By morning, everyone knew the shocking story. A military vehicle engaged in a rare nighttime exercise stopped on a gravel road with its headlights off and was invisible to Jackie and her friend, Paul Crosier, on the motorcycle. The resulting collision injured Paul and took Jackie's life. All of us at Ukarumpa felt the loss. We prayed. We asked why. We offered sympathy. Then we attended the sad funeral where they buried Jackie on a tree-shaded hill within the borders of Ukarumpa. She would not be forgotten.

Before long, her parents, Jack and Chick, gathered their three daughters and two sons and left Ukarumpa, with heavy hearts, for time alone as a family. They chose a coconut plantation along the shore of the Pacific Ocean. Surrounded by palms and cocoa trees with a long stretch of white sand and the eastern horizon, the family was blessed by God with the beginnings of healing. They knew their daughter and sister was in heaven with her beloved Jesus, but they missed her lively personality here and now. They walked along the sandy shore and discovered a narrow rivulet flowing out to the ocean. Turning inland, they walked up the stream until it got deeper and became a river, causing them to think about Dr. Redpath's word picture and, of course, Jackie. Their memories blended with the message heard before Easter.

Somber children returned to school and concerned parents went back to work, while bereaved Jack and Chick faced the condolences and questions of their Ukarumpa friends. To tell us more about their daughter Jackie's fatal accident, Chick agreed to speak at a planned women's get- together. We crowded into a large all-purpose room in the mission guesthouse, eager to uplift each other. Holding a worn leather diary that reflected her worn countenance, Chick stood to speak.

Halfway through her story, she told us that Jackie found Dr. Redpath's messages on the Holy Spirit from Ezekiel, chapter 47, deeply meaningful. Opening Jackie's diary, she read these words: "I'd like to pray for the spiritual gift of tongues, but I don't have the guts."

That's it! Nothing else in Jackie's writing registered in my mind. I hardly noticed when Chick finished and the women started to leave. I hustled out with one purpose—to get home and contemplate Jackie's words.

The house would be quiet. Jack had traveled to a distant village, and our three children would be asleep. With anticipation, I lit my kerosene lantern and hurried home downhill over the stony road. Inside the house, I checked on the children and then slipped quietly into our empty bedroom and sat on the edge of the bed.

Jackie wrote "guts," but I was too proper to use that term. Yet, I felt a kinship in her words "gift of tongues," while I wondered whether I even believed in the phenomenon. I remember when my sister-in-law Florence knelt and pleaded with God to help her become a better mother and found herself praying in an unknown language. She told her pastor, and he replied, "Satan can imitate 'tongues,' and no doubt that is what happened." Florence never again wanted anything to do with tongues. What about the brochure I recently received in the mail with angry red flames on the cover and the caption "Tongues—from God or Satan?"

All these thoughts were swirling through my mind, and even though I didn't have much knowledge or faith, I needed to settle this question. I wanted to know the truth of the Holy Spirit and whether I had the courage to open myself to the biblical reality of his presence. I prayed just to be "filled with the Spirit" and forget the gifts. However, I wanted to be a pure vessel for Jesus Christ, holy and creative.

I prayed for God to remove obstacles from my mind—the parts of my education and church life that ignored the role of the Holy Spirit. Also I handed over Florence's experience and prayed that whatever happened now would be from God and in no way from Satan. In short, I wanted to be rid of whatever kept me from opening myself to the Holy Spirit: education, pride, negative experiences, or just plain lack of "guts."

Suddenly, I perceived a vivid sense of entering a stream of gently flowing ankle-deep water. Beautiful fruit trees lined the banks. I kept walking until I noticed the water reaching my knees. It refreshed me. I eagerly and effortlessly walked on until the cool water reached my waist. The water ahead deepened. Abandoning all my fears, I unreservedly swam into the surrounding river until an invisible joy-filled Presence reached out a hand and guided me to the riverbank.

After that dreamlike experience, a specific desire to praise God overtook me. I spoke a few syllables, and before I finished, a rush of unknown words softly tumbled out of my unbelieving mouth.

I was praising God, prayerfully, in a very unusual but fluent language! Strangely, I didn't believe in spiritual gifts until then.

This realization removed all my doubts about the Holy Spirit of the Bible being the third person of the Trinity. His presence in me was complete. Transforming joy and faith accompanied my praying in a heavenly language. However, being unfamiliar with this new gift, I wondered, "If I stop speaking, will the gift disappear? Will I be able to pray like this when I wake up in the morning, or is this just a one-time occurrence?" So much to learn! Exhausted, I finally lay down on the bed and slept.

The next day, my schedule included flying out to join Jack in the Stucky's village, but I felt that I needed to share my gift, my joy, my exhilaration, with someone, privately but without delay. When my last child exited the door for school and I had "tested" my gift, I rushed up the hill to my trusted friend Aretta's house. She opened the door and looked quite surprised.

I burst out, "Guess what happened to me last night?"

"Good or bad?" she asked.

"Rapturous! Life changing! I prayed to be filled with the Holy Spirit after Chick read Jackie's diary, and I was not only filled but also given a spiritual gift."

"That's great," Aretta affirmed, "and I believe it, but I thought you didn't think you needed anything more."

"Oh, Aretta, I didn't believe it, but I'm a believer now. I just didn't have the 'guts'!" We both laughed and hugged. I returned home satisfied.

I left the children with missionary friends and flew in the single-engine Cessna to join Jack and visit Al and Dellene Stucky up in the mountains. As we touched down, I spotted Jack and realized how much I had missed him. After hugs and greetings all around, we climbed into their dusty station wagon to enjoy a scenic ride to the picturesque village.

L. Bass

When the Stuckys were not busy translating, they loved to cook and bake on their wood stove. After a tasty dinner, we shared friendly conversation until bedtime. A six-foot-high woven bamboo wall separated two small bedrooms. I climbed into our bed, snuggled close to Jack, and whispered in his ear, "I have something to tell you, but I don't want to wake our friends in the next room."

From Chick's diary reading to my life-changing encounter, I whispered it all out to him. After the part about the water to swim in, he said, "That's very significant. It was a baptism, a spiritual baptism." Acts 1:5 reads, "John baptized with water, but in a few days you will be baptized with the Holy Spirit."

Yes, Jack was right! I hadn't used those words to describe my infilling, but I had no doubt that I had experienced a baptism. Together, we quietly rejoiced in this newly given grace and then dropped off to sleep.

Sitting in the back of the single-engine Cessna on our return flight to Ukarumpa, I mulled over the recent events. *How was I different now?*

Would I be giving the church prophetic messages in this new language? No—God's Spirit within assured me. Rather, this gift was for private devotions to God. "I will pray with my Spirit but pray also with my mind," says 1 Corinthians 14:15. *Would God continue to use my gift of creativity to put spiritual truth into visual form? Would this empowerment change the Louise Bass who existed? Would I be the same "me" who had trouble explaining things with words, who shrank from social encounters, and who always thought her artistic efforts were inferior?* With God's help, I wanted to be an obedient, useful, caring Christian.

With thoughts of the recent past and Jackie's accidental death, I sensed God disclosing a humbling revelation to me through John 12:24: "Unless a kernel of wheat falls to the ground and dies, it remains only a single seed. But if it dies, it produces many seeds." I'm sure Jackie never imagined when she wrote in her diary that some day she would be planting seeds. As the plane descended toward a grassy strip and the mission pilot maneuvered it to a gentle landing at Ukarumpa, my thoughts ascended to new heights as I wondered what the future held for us.

8

CATASTROPHIC CHANGES

Rainy season blew in the same day Jack and I flew in to Ukarumpa from the Stuckys'. Our barefoot young teenagers, carrying their shoes and lunch boxes, sloshed through the puddles, happy we were home. When everyone dried out, we heard about occurrences in the children's home and upcoming events at school. Jonathan and his classmates were practicing to sing in Handel's *Messiah*; Joye had a part in the chorus of *The Mikado* operetta that required sewing a costume; Jackie learned a part for the play *Silas Marner*. We appreciated the conscientious volunteer teachers in our schools who were educating our young people.

As predictable as the change from rainy season to dry, change hung on the horizon for the New Guinea government. In 1973, self-government peacefully became law. In 1975, the final separation from the British monarchy was scheduled. Activities included a traditional ceremony in Goroka, a centrally located town. Surrounding a large grass soccer field, a wooden fence festooned with colorful leaves

and flowers provided the local people with a place to watch the show. On one side of the oval, a canopied grandstand awaited the seating of officials and honored dignitaries. The royal guests, Queen Elizabeth II and her husband, Prince Philip, advanced toward the chairs, which served as thrones. A deafening outcry thundered across the field. The Queen looked regal in her summer ensemble. However, Prince Philip won the crowd's attention, as he was attired in an immaculate white military uniform and wearing a tall headdress with cascading pure white bird plumage, the symbol of an esteemed chieftain and the envy of every tribesman.

Drums began to pulsate as barefoot dancers stomped to a jungle beat. Local males, wearing sarongs, leaves, shells, and fur pelts, advanced in various formations. Another group appeared displaying large and elaborate headdresses of orange, yellow, green, and black bird-of-paradise feathers. Disguised by enormous clay masks, a troop of highland Asaro mud-men dancers carried long menacing spears and made mock thrusts at the "enemy." Next, a bevy of bare-breasted women shuffled and swayed to the hypnotic music of bamboo flutes and Jew's harps.

The New Guineans knew how to stage a peaceful demonstration! When the dust settled, these diverse tribal people had their independence. Soon the northeastern half of the island of New Guinea joined Papua on the southeast, and, together, they became the nation of Papua New Guinea (PNG). The western half of the island belonged to Indonesia and underwent several name and ownership changes over the years.

Change also affected the Bass family. For Jonathan and 16 classmates, high school graduation meant celebration and separation. The graduates packed their memories and said farewell to their families and homeland to take flight to a new and unfamiliar world. Lonely parents left the airstrip, empty and anxious, praying for safety, wisdom, and faith for their offspring. Jack and I felt certain that our son, going to live with his Aunt Audrey and Uncle Mike in Michigan, would find guidance, security, and love.

Dependable Jonathan soon enrolled in a community college and worked a part-time job. After a year and a half, he bought a car, drove to California, and flew back to Papua New Guinea to connect with friends and help us pack for our third furlough. Joye's graduation coincided with our plans. We packed papers, photos, and keepsakes for shipping; stored our belongings; and leased out our house for the next year. Joye's application to attend Taylor University in Indiana was accepted for the fall semester. Jack's application to train as a chaplain at Detroit's Sinai Grace Hospital, for a future retirement career, was accepted. We had all our ducks in a row!

As a family we traveled from PNG by air to California, where Jonathan's car waited. Feeling like the Beverly Hillbillies, we loaded the car trunk and roof with most of our worldly possessions and drove east until we saw the "Welcome to Michigan" sign. After warm-hearted greetings with parents, siblings, and friends in Detroit, we made a plan. With Jonathan settled in Traverse City, and Joye with us for two more weeks, we would stay with my parents in Detroit until lodgings were found near the hospital teaching Jack's course and a high school for Jackie to attend.

On August 20, 1979, Jack and I were given my parents' spare bedroom while Joye and Jackie climbed the stairs to sleep in their grandparents' attic. Early the next morning, before the sun was up, I sensed Jack getting up and starting to dress. Since early-morning jogging was his habit, I rolled over and went back to sleep. Later, I don't know how long after, my mother pushed open the bedroom door and yelled out, "Come quickly! Jack's lying on the floor of the garage!" My first thought was, *He's probably praying!* But I grabbed a robe and hurried outside. The car door was open, where he had evidently sat down to rest and then fell forward onto the floor.

A shockwave of disbelief washed over me. My dad gave him CPR but, I knew Jack was lifeless. I needed to tell the girls. I ran back to the house and up the stairs to wake them. They quickly followed me back downstairs. Their father, my husband, was gone. This couldn't be happening! He was only 51.

When we returned to the backyard, the police had arrived and laid Jack on the driveway surface and were trying to resuscitate him. Finally, an ambulance came to rush him to the hospital, and I was told to wait in the house for a phone call. My thoughts blurred. Time stood still. I tried to visualize Jack alive but could only see him lying on the ground in his favorite brown and black striped sweater.

My soul mate, my partner, my dearest friend—we were one. Take away half and what's left? I had been reduced to half a person. As partners, we complemented each other, assisted each other, and encouraged each other serving our mighty God in Papua New Guinea. I knew I couldn't handle this catastrophe.

As a 49-year-old widow, I was distraught beyond words, knowing I'd probably end up in a mental hospital, of no use to anybody. Initially, I was overwhelmed—mentally and spiritually. I didn't blame God, but I was so bewildered and confused that I failed to recognize or call upon the Comforter living within me.

My grieving parents sat us down at the kitchen table to try to comfort the girls and me. They offered me coffee that went untouched. Still numb, Joye and Jackie went upstairs and dressed. The hospital called to officially confirm Jack's death. It was time to choose a funeral home. A God-given realization enabled me to know that I indeed did have the inner strength to cope with this tragedy. Didn't my spiritual baptism prepare me for this?

Then, gently, as if waiting for me to acknowledge him, the Holy Spirit brought to mind these words, "Even though I walk through the valley of the shadow of death, I will fear no evil, for you are with me; your rod and your staff, they comfort me" Psalm 23:4. God-given, these were powerful words of reassurance, comforting words to quiet my fears, confirming words of God's sufficiency. I realized fully where

Jack was. I could now embrace peace in knowing he had been "translated" and rested safely with the Lord Jesus.

At the funeral in Beulah Baptist Church, people crowded in to honor Jack's life. It was packed. Jonathan, with my sister, Audrey, and her husband, Mike, drove down from northern Michigan; cousins drove over from Canada; and coworkers flew in from Dallas. Likewise, back at Ukarumpa, there was a special service to honor Jack. Many friends sent their tributes and sympathies.

Rosemary Young, an Australian translator's wife wrote: "Jack cannot be replaced. He was a special and unique creation. And you cannot help but miss him and sometimes wish he were still with you … I think all of us at Ukarumpa are the richer for Jack's pilgrimage among us. He never sought prominence, yet in many ways he led us all. Jack had a rare blend of true humility and real godliness. No wonder the Lord called him home. He was ready."

Ger Reesink, a Dutchman, our friend and director, wrote: "I've been encouraged so often, almost purified by the conversations that Jack and I have had, when he shared his insights, wondering about their implications, wondering, too, how much of it was God's truth. He knows now, firsthand information is available to him. He doesn't even have to raise his hands trying to reach out to God; they are together, because his task here—apparently—was finished. Finished? And what about Louise and Jonathan, Joye and Jackie, what about me and so many others who were privileged to call him friend? I asked God, my and your Father, why can't I talk with Jack anymore? Jack understood me. I was not afraid to tell him how I felt or what I thought because he stood not ready with his judgment but with open love and wonder."

In short, our loss was enormously indescribable. However, I was grateful to God for his marvelous timing. He had prepared me for my solo life. He had enabled me to be alert to my need for being filled with his Spirit. He knew I would need empowering and comforting as never before. He knew I would need a deep, dependable relationship with his Spirit for what now faced me. What if I had ignored the nudges God had used to alert me to the need for a relationship with the Holy Spirit? Where would I be now without the strength, faith, and guidance of God's Holy Spirit? How good and gracious my God was for going before to prepare and enable me to walk through the valley of the shadow of death accompanied by Father, Son, and Holy Spirit.

My practical needs and the many challenges for the days ahead didn't disappear. Questions raced through my mind. "Where will we live now? How can I move Joye to Taylor University in Indiana? Where will Jackie attend high school? Where will I secure finances after leaving our mission? Will I find work? Can I continue to serve God?" In the days, months, and years ahead, I saw hurdles miraculously and compassionately removed and help provided.

Packing the car and driving to Upland, Indiana, were supposed to be Jack's jobs. Now, just days after the funeral, the four of us worked together to jam-pack Joye's luggage into our used car and squeeze in like sardines. Jonathan drove. We arrived without incident. While Jonathan and Jackie helped Joye set up her dorm room, I found my way to the parents' orientation meeting. Looking over the spacious auditorium, I saw twosomes, husbands and wives sitting closely side-by-side as they prepared to leave their child. Panic struck. Could I walk into a row of seats and sit down next to an empty space? Oh, how I missed Jack. I sat down and cried, feeling unattached and very lonely.

That's how my grief played out, one lonely situation at a time, while God's Holy Spirit in me waited gently until I was ready to summon him as my Helper.

9

LEARNING GOD'S PROVISION

Everything about college life was brand new and exhilarating for Joye. The sorrow of losing her father diminished as the newness of country, culture, and college consumed her. She took a part-time job serving in the school cafeteria. Her Ukarumpa T-shirt became a conversation piece, and one mealtime a bright young student named Jack liked what he saw. His curiosity about a place named Ukarumpa and a lovely girl named Joye led to friendship and love.

The rest of us settled in Traverse City, MI. Jonathan completed college, and Jackie entered senior high school. Always praying about our tomorrows, we watched God faithfully provide our daily bread and a roof over our heads. A quaint white bungalow next to a church by the Bay of Lake Michigan became our home and family gathering place after the shock of losing our beloved father and husband. Our lives seemed empty without Jack's love, wisdom, and strength, but we had each other and the Lord.

The next hurdle took the shape of a dollar sign. Or was it a question mark: "Finances?" Previously, our Detroit church's support funds went to the Wycliffe mission headquarters in California. From there they paid for travel, living needs, and other expenses. Also while in New Guinea, we kept a small account for buying groceries, paying language helpers, and other incidentals. Now, in Michigan, our financial requirements were much more complicated. I needed money for our rent, utilities, transportation, clothing essentials, household necessities, and food. These needs were the topics of many thoughts and prayers. One fanciful notion went like this: *I want to do artwork, but I'm unfamiliar with the latest graphic trends and don't feel qualified. I know God will provide for us, but how? Perhaps, as I'm out walking, he'll drop a $10,000 bill onto my path to take care of our needs.* Ridiculous! I soon realized God in his consistent generosity would continue to provide abundantly in his blueprint for our lives.

His continuing care for us became clear. First, a young couple bought our modest Papua New Guinea home at Ukarumpa and I was enabled to make a down payment on a more comfortable, suitable home in Traverse City. This experience helped me realize how prized our homes are to us. I wondered whether Michigan homeowners would buy pen-and-ink drawings of their homes. As a trial, I exhibited a few sample drawings at an art show in a local mall. It was a success!

Optimistically, I entered other art fairs with my display pieces and camera and took orders and addresses. After closings, I drove to the picturesque houses, snapped photos, and then sketched them in my spare room "studio." What a creative God we serve! Well aware that my ability to draw came from God, I thanked Father, Son, and Holy Spirit for not only equipping me but also leading me into this new art venture. Again, he proved the truth of his words written in Philippians 4:19: "And my God will meet all your needs according to His glorious riches in Christ Jesus."

However, the financial challenges continued. Our property tax deadline loomed closer, and I discovered that I needed another hundred dollars to pay this crucial bill. Scanning the newspaper, I noticed articles about the annual Traverse City Cherry Festival to be held on the waterfront. Advertisements told of a new attraction offering cash awards: a chalk drawing competition, to be rendered on a cement retaining wall near the sandy beach. Eager to enter, I made some sketches and decided to represent an arched doorway apparently opened through the wall with a young couple looking into the view beyond.

When I arrived, an official pointed out my portion of the wall, standing five feet high and five feet wide. The other contestants were busily drawing, and I joined them with my box of colored chalks. The young man on my left had his picture half finished, a waterfall with cherries spilling over it. He told me he was the best artist there and came from another city to show off his talent. *Hmm*, I thought.

I finished creating my chalk archway scene just in time to see a group of three officials walking up to each artist's illustration and conversing among themselves. Eagerly, I awaited their visit to my section of the wall. To my utter dismay, when they finished with the "waterfall artist," they walked right past my beautiful picture. I was flabbergasted! Without even discussing it, they continued on to look at the girl's work on my right. Their dismissal of my work was so disappointing. No comments. No suggestions. No acknowledgment.

Fighting rejection, I gathered up my chalks to head home. Then, I heard a judge call for all the artists to gather on the central sidewalk. Crestfallen, I sauntered to the edge of the avid group and listened half-heartedly as he called out the name of the third-place winner, the second-place winner (no waterfall artist yet …), and, then, the first-place winner—Louise Bass! *What? Yes!* Unbelievably, I won! God went before me. I worked. He supplied. Ecstatically, I thanked the judge for the $100 check; silently, with a heart of gratitude and love, I thanked my Heavenly Father for providing my tax money—the exact amount I needed of course.

That incident prompted me to recall how God had equipped me with creative artistry skills, through which he directed my productivity and generously met our financial needs. This provision had occurred dramatically so often in my life that I wondered whether creativity is also a Spirit-given gift. Thinking of examples in the Bible, I remembered God giving Moses the design for the tabernacle in Exodus chapter 31, which reads, "See I have chosen Bezalel … and I have filled him with the Spirit of God, with skill, ability and knowledge in all kinds of crafts—to make artistic designs." It seemed like "creativity" could be added to the list of spiritual gifts in Romans 12 and 1 Corinthians 12.

From my experience, I believe I received a natural talent to create visual art. Later, as I allowed the Holy Spirit to enable me, the gift was enhanced and expanded to serve God. Graciously, throughout my life in very specific ways, God miraculously provided for me and for my family through the use of this spiritual enablement.

Mulling over the evidence of the other spiritual gifts mentioned in the New Testament, I noticed some unique differences. Compared to preaching, teaching, or counseling, visual art is not usually fulfilled in person-to-person encounters. Instead, someone in Mexico may learn to read from an illustrated primer. A person in Thailand may silently comprehend a Northern Khmer Bible passage by observing the illustrations. The Holy Spirit, giver of gifts, knows our personalities exactly and precisely enables us to find fulfillment as we desire to reach others for Jesus Christ by our words, our drawings, our music, our writing, or our other skills.

> *"One individual has definite or special talent*
> *for expressing in some medium,*
> *what other personalities can hear,*
>   *see,*
>   *smell,*
>   *feel,*
>   *taste,*
>   *understand,*
>   *enjoy,*
>   *be stimulated by,*
>   *be involved in,*
>   *find refreshment in,*
>   *find satisfaction in,*
>   *find fulfillment in,*
>   *experience reality in,*
>   *be agonized by, be pleased by,*
>   *enter into,*
> *but which they could not produce themselves.*
> *Art satisfies and fulfills something in the person creating and in*
> *those responding."*
>
> — *FROM HIDDEN ART*, BY EDITH SCHAEFFER

My interest in Dr. Francis Schaeffer's books led to discovering his wife Edith's writing. Her expressions and explanations helped me understand the relationship between the visual artist and the viewer. Her insight brought confirmation in my spirit of the sensitive ministering of God's Spirit to others through art. Though satisfaction or fulfillment might be delayed or not even perceived personally in many forms of artwork, Bible-based chalk drawings sometimes bring an immediate response from viewers. God often uses our eyes as the gateway to our spirits.

I noticed that when others observed chalk drawings, they often realized a strong spiritual message and wanted to reply in some way. This encouraged me. Because of this effect of God's powerful Spirit engaging viewers during the drawing, I was eager to accept invitations to draw in local churches. Carefully, I prepared, practiced, and prayed for the audience and asked the Lord to show me a visual theme to meet the needs of each particular group. His answers were out of this world! Artistic ideas flowed from my Creator into my mind and out through my fingers.

A phone call came from a Traverse City church asking me to speak and draw for a women's gathering. My inspiration came from the Old Testament book of Esther.

> *"On the third day Esther put on her royal robes and stood in the inner court of the palace, in front of the king's hall. The king was sitting on his royal throne in the hall, facing the entrance. When he saw Queen Esther standing in the court, he was pleased with her and held out to her the golden scepter that was in his hand. So the king asked, "What is it, Queen Esther? What is your request? Even up to half the kingdom, it will be given to you."*
>
> — ESTHER 5:1-3

That was a crucial moment in history for this brave Jewish queen, so I knew my chalk drawing must depict courage. Could I do it? On the evening of the presentation, the auditorium filled quickly with women eager to see the drawing take form. After a brief introduction, the overhead fluorescent lights dimmed while I turned up the spotlights to display a seemingly blank paper-covered board. I began to draw. As a background, majestic columns with purple draperies and carpets were quickly sketched in. Then, I added a royal throne and drew King Xerxes seated and extending the golden scepter to his approaching wife. The beautiful Queen Esther slowly came to life, adorned in richly colored silken robes and sparkling jewels. Cautiously, I portrayed her graceful hand reaching out to touch the tip of the royal scepter.

Before the meeting, I had drawn Jesus on the board with "invisible" chalk that would appear when (undetected) I deftly switched on the overhead ultraviolet light. At the exact moment I completed the queen's redeeming touch, the figure of Jesus appeared. The king was overshadowed. Jesus, the true husband-king, welcomed Esther, enabling her, and empowering her, to save the lives of her Hebrew people and the lives of the women in the auditorium. Effective dramatic power was suddenly released. His Word was made visible. "Not by might nor by power, but by my Spirit, says the Lord Almighty" Zechariah 4:6. Ancient words visibly depicted. Ever true!

A holy hush fell upon the audience. Silence reigned. Not sure what to do next, I quietly stood waiting by the chalkboard for an opportune time to close in prayer and pack up. Then, peering through the darkness, I observed God's Spirit moving in the auditorium. I saw some women kneeling, several were prostrate on the floor, a few were crying, and one young woman was sobbing and sobbing. I whispered, "Oh, Lord, help me," as I stepped down from the low stage and made my way to the woman who was weeping uncontrollably.

"Can I be of any help?" I asked tentatively.

With some difficulty, she regained her composure, enabling her to say, "For a long time, I believed the Lord Jesus wanted me to work for him in Africa, and as I reached out like Esther, he accepted me and opened the way for me to go."

I thanked the Lord and later heard that she did indeed go to serve Jesus Christ in Africa. Amazing to me was this picture I had never drawn before or since, but I knew it was the very one he wanted for that assembly. God's Spirit moves explicitly for specific purposes to edify and direct the Body of Christ, his people.

Twenty-five years later, when this book was being written, Pam, a stranger to me, introduced herself to me in a writer's group. After she asked whether I remembered when I spoke and drew Queen Esther's story, I said, "Oh, yes!" Then, Pam related this memory. When she was a troubled newlywed adjusting to her new role, concerned about her marriage and bewildered, a friend invited her to a Christian women's meeting. "Come with me and see a woman artist rendering a complete chalk-drawing right before your eyes," she coaxed. Pam went, listened, and watched, and God worked a miracle.

As our eyes met 25 years later, she told me that God used the portrayal of Esther's acceptance and that evening's experience to show her that he loved her and would give her whatever she needed to have a strong and loving marriage. *Fulfill her marriage? How could colored chalk marks on a board achieve this wondrous work in Pam's life?* However, this is how the Spirit of God works! I've discovered that even when we are cautiously willing to use the skills he gives us, we are empowered by the Holy Spirit, his will is done, hearts are changed, and we are gratified. There is no joy, no other satisfaction, quite like it. Pam's testimony, given to me years later, encouraged my soul. Doing his work is like sampling a spiritual fruit salad and tasting "love, joy, peace, patience, kindness, goodness, faithfulness, gentleness, and self control" Galatians 5:22-23.

10
INSIDE AFRICA

For more than 19 years I served God by creating visual art in New Guinea yet now wondered whether I would be given new opportunities to work in the "ends of the earth." In 1990, it seemed very unlikely, but I still wanted to serve. My children, now grown, had all married their sweethearts. Jonathan met Jackie O'Brien at church in Traverse City, Joye met Jack Judy at Taylor University, and Jackie met Dan Dillinger at a church picnic in Grand Rapids. As much as I wanted my offspring to have happy marriages and their own families, occasionally, my mother's heart felt purposeless and empty.

A minister once said, "The loneliest place you can be is to wake up Christmas morning in an empty house." Yet it happened more than once in the winter when the young families awoke to impassable roads or sick children. My motherly duties changed, and I gave advice only when asked, prayed for them often, and loved them dearly. God blessed us as a family, yet, nonetheless, I still sensed the Holy Spirit tapping my shoulder to get my attention. Nudging. Prodding.

What did my future hold? I still longed to use my artwork to benefit remote people—but where, when, and how? I needed answers. Reading Isaiah in the Old Testament, I came across this mandate in chapter 54, verse 2:

> *"Enlarge the place of your tent*
> *Stretch your tent curtains wide.*
> *Do not hold back;*
> *Lengthen your cords,*
> *Strengthen your stakes."*

My home in northern Michigan was comfortable but "unstretchable"; the "cords and stakes" held me tight. I knew God wanted me to use the spiritual gifts he had endowed me with, but I needed specific directions. It felt like I sat down with a brush in my hand to paint on an empty white canvas and a small, nagging inner voice discouraged me with fears, such as *Who do you think you are? You can't even draw—let alone paint* and *Without Jack's wisdom and stability, you can't do it* and *You can't leave your children and grandchildren.*

The thoughts taunted me. Doubts sometimes disturbed me, causing me to think I had it all wrong. Fears held me back: *Maybe I should forget enlarging the place of my tent. I must choose.* Finally, a positive plan began to materialize: *I'll pray to my Father in heaven asking him to show me clearly how I can fulfill his desires for me. I will share my seeking with nobody else. I'll just wait for an answer.* It would be my secret.

It wasn't three weeks after this decision that I received an airmail letter with a Kenyan stamp. *Who did I know in Africa?* The return address belonged to my Papua New Guinea friends Ed and Aretta Loving, who were now stationed in Nairobi, Kenya, with Bible Translation and Literacy.

> *Dear Louise,*
>
> *How are you? We're doing well but very busy. There's a young Dutchman here, Roel, who is illustrating literacy books. He's swamped. Could you come to Nairobi and help with the artwork? Let us know soon.*
>
> *Love, Aretta*

Open up those tent curtains—I'm going to Kenya! Sometimes people wanting to follow Jesus are afraid he might call them to ominous Africa, so they stay home and miss out. Since college prayer-times, I pleaded with God on behalf of the African people. This must be where God wanted me. I would surely miss Jack when I traveled overseas, but I would not "hold back." The paperwork came promptly; I gathered a few old skirts and tops to wear and departed from Detroit on Air Zambia, bound for Africa. Soon, from my window seat, I was gazing down on the green broccoli-like jungles of Africa, and I surrendered to this land and people I loved.

Disembarking from the plane in Nairobi, I located my luggage in the steamy waiting room, which was pungent with unfamiliar spicy floral scents and warm body aromas. One of my luggage-locks was cut, and my sandals and small paint box were missing, but three months of adventure were awaiting me on this vast continent with wide-open tent flaps.

My first job in the publishing department of the Wycliffe mission involved producing literacy booklets for new readers in Kenya, Tanzania, and Sudan. The African Bible Society had printed a series of biblical storybooks with narrow horizontal pictures fitted across the top or bottom of the pages. Alterations were needed now to fit a new vertical page format. Most of the Bible characters were drawn from the knees up, so my job involved adding legs and feet. After inking in about 25 pairs of sandals, I joked that each pair was a "Bass Sandal" original!

When *you* tell the Lord God *you* will obey him, will *you* draw sandals? Probably not! You may teach eager children, provide health care to hurting people, sing the national anthem in a large stadium, act in a drama that reflects your standards, or ... the sky's the limit. For me, drawing sandals offered an opportunity to help new readers grasp God's message in the Bible.

"How would you like to fly to the northern desert near Ethiopia to illustrate literacy books for the Rendile people?" asked the person in charge.

"Well ... ah ... yes," I stammered. "Tell me more."

I learned about the tall, angular nomadic Rendile people, related to the renowned Masai Desert tribe. They moved their camels, sheep, and goats ("shoats" for those who can't tell them apart) regularly to forage for water and food. They subsisted on goat's milk sometimes laced with camel blood taken from camels' carotid arteries. Literacy books would rely heavily on stories of camels, sheep, and goats. I would travel to the desert to learn the customs and surroundings of the tribe's people. Living near them, taking photographs, and sketching people and animals would provide details and cultural knowledge all necessary for authentic drawings.

Without warning, a colossal problem loomed on the sandy horizon. The open-doors for outsiders to photograph the Rendile camels were now closed. The edict prohibiting camel photography came about when two tourists left their vehicle to get photos of a camel herd. Unaware of the Rendile belief that photographing female camels caused sterility, they ignored the nearby shepherd's warnings. Both photographers were speared to death!

"Oh, Lord," I implored him, "have I followed you all this way to be banned from my subject matter?"

It looked hopeless. I settled back at the figurative—and literal—drawing board and attempted to adjust to this setback. The next day, Ed Loving entered the studio and announced, "A man from the Canadian government just arrived in Nairobi to inspect the camel-herds Canada donated to the nomads during a famine." He added, "There's an empty seat on the two-seater mission plane, and we booked you a place to accompany the government official. Be sure to take your camera; he's carrying one." Miraculous!

We soared low under cloud cover with a hawk's-eye view of central Kenya. Resembling a sand carpet, the desert stretched from north to south with an occasional circular pattern of thorn bush animal enclosures. The airstrip at Knorr was indefinable except for two rows of sandy stones marking the edges. Amazingly, our jungle pilot touched down right in front of the missionary's solitary A-frame home. We were greeted by Nick and Lynn Swanepoel, a young South African couple who braved the dry, stinging winds and scarcity of water and food to translate the Bible into the Rendile language. I soon settled into a peaked upper room away from the elements.

From my diary entry, March 4, 1990:

*Morning woke me at 6:30 a.m. to a clear blue sky; the sun beat
me up! Took a shower in cold well-water carried by straight-
backed chattering women. Mouth watering aromas led to the
kitchen where Lynn served bacon, eggs, papaya, and tea. Afterward, my young guide shepherded me into the desert strewn
with sharp rocks and thorns to see a herd of camels not yet on
distant grazing ground. Grumbling adult camels and fuzzy
wide-eyed calves were corralled inside thorn bush enclosures.
People? They lived in small igloo-shaped tents of animal skins
fastened to long, curved saplings. My guide took me inside his
tent to introduce his mother, bare breasted, squatting by a small
fire of precious firewood. Camel milk in gourds hung on poles.
She offered me some in a tin cup. Yuck! What to do? It might
be sour or contain blood! As soon as I told the boy to say "no
thanks," I immediately regretted it and said, "OK, just a little."
Surprise, the milk tasted fresh, sweet, and kind of smoky. She
was neat, but because of no water, she burned the inside of the
gourds to clean them.*

Sunday swirled in, and I gathered my sketchbook, pencils, and camera,
dropped them into my shoulder bag, and ventured out alone. Looking
for a landmark, I saw nothing but sandy ground, thorns, and rocks.
After walking gingerly for a while, I saw what appeared to be a small
church in the distance. If this weren't a mirage, I would sketch it. Far
enough away to be unnoticed, I found a medium-sized boulder where
I could sit. Within minutes, a group of excited children appeared from
nowhere and stopped to stare at me. What happened next is written
in this poem.

SCORPIONS AND LEOPARDS

In the thorn-spiked Kenyan desert,
I sit on a stool-sized boulder,
And sketch a half-empty church.
Where are the people?
Do they worship Jesus?
Truant brown children
Gather round me on gazelles' feet.
They come to see a human,
With pink skin and gold teeth,
Who sits where the scorpions hide.
Their pure Swahili phrases,
I cannot translate.
I search for a word and say "chui."
The chatter increases.
A "leopard" forms on my sketchpad.
Now the children sing words I know.
Words learned by rote.
"Bind us togeda, Lord. Bind us togeda."
(With cords of language, cords of music,)
Cords of Love.

The leopard ("chui") sketch became the passport into the kingdom of these children. The Holy Spirit's empowered gift of art helped to cross language barriers, and I knew for this reason he entrusted it to me.

One day, a brown-skinned, grizzle-bearded Rendile man in a derby hat and red sarong entered the Swanepoel's home. Nick addressed him as "Father-in-Law." He was a character! Posing for a sketch, he told jokes in his language. The young men in the room chuckled. Nick interpreted when the old man asked me to look for his big toe in Nairobi. It was lost in an auto accident in the capital city, and he was fortunate to lose only one. Working on brown paper, I sketched a big toe complete with toenail and gave it to him. He cackled and thought it a huge joke. Then he slipped the drawing into his sandal along with his other four toes. His toe was restored!

The married women wore decorative necklaces that extended from chin to collarbone. They refused to be photographed, but I found a way to record their adornment. Nick got permission for me to paint a portrait of one young woman, and I sat opposite her at the kitchen table with a small set of oil paints, a brush, and a small canvas-board. My model was a patient sitter. When I finished, she and many onlookers held the painting, examined it, and turned it over to locate the rest of her body. After the painting session, the women seemed to accept me. They presented me with a colorful handcrafted necklace—a token of their friendship. Artwork again eased the barriers and differences between us.

Back in Nairobi, I used the photos as references to make drawings for reading books from a series created by Roel. Also on my drawing desk lay illustrated alphabet charts in two languages belonging to Kenyans teaching literacy classes.

Please, Lord, I prayed between jobs, *I'd love to go on a safari.* This is how it happened: the Lovings planned an off-road expedition in a four-wheel-drive vehicle to locate and recruit unemployed teachers and offer literacy jobs. Thankfully, I was included in their safari. We drove over grasslands, through rivers, and up rocky inclines. Menacing nail strips and gun-toting officials stopped us temporarily, as did Cape buffalo, one of Africa's most dangerous animals. High up on the river banks, we marveled at the speed of the crocodiles below, as they patrolled the river's edge. Ed took us into many small villages where friendly people sat, talked to us in adequate English, and offered bottles of warm Coke to drink. Such an exciting way to explore Kenya! My creative juices were active, and I drew many sketches for future use.

Maralal
Kenya

I was sorry to see my departure date arrive but packed my stuff and prepared to leave the guesthouse, my friends, and Africa. Tapping sounded at the door, and I opened it to see Dr. Katy Barnwell, director of translations for Wycliffe Bible Translators. I invited her inside but wondered why she wanted to see me. She had heard I made detailed pen-and-ink drawings and asked to see samples of my work. Several postcards with drawings of Michigan lighthouses were in my travel bag, and I handed them to her.

She considered them carefully and then spoke: "Part of my job is to find a pen-and-ink artist to work in conjunction with the British Bible Society adding new illustrations to an existing set used in Bibles around the world. Would you be interested in doing Bible illustrations?"

I laughed and said, "No, if I ever drew the Holy Land, I would have to see it firsthand, but I've never been to Israel."

I thought I had turned her down gracefully, but Katy responded, "Pray about it, and let me know your answer tomorrow."

Alone in my room, I did not need to spend much time praying; I knew God wanted me to do those illustrations. I sensed that the pen-and-ink technique I perfected was ready to be used beyond my Michigan studio. Maybe Katy would agree to let me work in London, where museums would undoubtedly contain reference material on Israel.

In the morning, Katy returned for my answer. I said, "Yes, but …," and before I could tell her about London, she took my answer as a yes and said, "Fine! We want to send you to the Institute of Holy Land Studies [now the Jerusalem University College]."

"Where's that?" I innocently asked.

"In Jerusalem, on Mount Zion," she answered to my unbelieving ears.

11

ISRAELI EXPEDITION

Never in all my travels did I yearn to go to Israel, but in July 1991, I was on my way to Jerusalem. Flying into the Ben Gurion Airport in Tel Aviv, I witnessed some of the destruction left from the missile attacks that had occurred during the Gulf War. That war had ended in February of 1991, but people were not yet encouraged to travel in Israel. However, as an illustrator and not just a tourist, I needed to see the land firsthand to dispel my idea of the Holy Land as a two-dimensional felt background upon which equally flat biblical characters were placed.

I rode on a bus to Jerusalem and enrolled in the Institute of Holy Land Studies, where I would attend a six-week biblical geography course. Built in 1853, the building stood on Mt. Zion, and the institute moved there in 1967 with the purpose of teaching the historical background of the Word of God in its natural setting. Volumes of history resided in its massive walls. Its architectural distinctions of arched doorways and stone stairwells made it the perfect place to learn about ancient biblical chronicles and the notable geography of Israel.

Inspired by this optimal environment, I became an eager student. My fellow classmates were mostly young Christian seminary students from various countries. They came to study Bible background and experience the revered center of their faith. Almost daily, a Palestinian bus took us on a field trip.

Our knowledgeable institute lecturers often taught us from the front of the bus as we traveled south to the Sinai Peninsula and north to the Syrian border. I discovered that much of Israel had not changed since biblical times. On our frequent field trips, our driver took us over rocky desert roads where woolly sheep grazed near the black goatskin tents of the Bedouin shepherds.

Tour bus lectures and experimental land-lessons were both extraordinarily interesting and sensually stimulating. I tasted the famed salt of the Dead Sea when we stopped to take a not-so-refreshing dip in the heavy, buoyant water. Driving north, we saw the orange groves of the kibbutzim and sampled the sweet, juicy fruit. Back on clamoring Jerusalem streets, we were greeted to the smell of roasting lamb-kebobs wafting from curbside vendors, and the harsh blasts of the shofar alerted us to the rabbis' celebrations. Our guide helped us see beyond the bus station and MacDavid's Kosher Burgers to the windy Hinnon valley. For me, time stood still.

My alerted senses took it all in and expanded these Holy Land impressions to forever change my ideas of Israel. I began to perceive things with my heart as the Holy Spirit enlightened my vision. In retrospect, I knew I was preparing to create the illustrations I had been commissioned to draw. By allowing the landscape, the history, the culture, and the essence of this holiest of lands to enter my eyes and merge with my artistic spirit, God was enabling me to adorn his Word with accurate explanatory drawings and scenes of Israel and its people.

Before our eager group started out on a field trip, the teacher showed us maps to orient us to the area of study: the Negev Desert, Masada, Capernaum, Bethlehem, Caesarea, etc. The entire land of

Israel is geographically small, 265 miles north to south and only 70 miles east to west. Our field-trips covered most of the territory.

Often, our destination was an archeological dig. One morning our bus labored up a steep hill to a flat place where our teacher directed us to sit, in the warm sun, on a low stone wall. There before us, the ever-present rocks formed orderly grids on the ancient ground. "The foundation of Herod's palace," I scribbled in my sketchbook. The rectangular chamber held an ancient cistern and burnt-sienna clay jars identifying the archaic cooking area. At dig after dig, I faithfully recorded these facts and studied for the inevitable quiz.

The uniformity of these archeological sites blurred their importance in my mind. What I really wanted to see were three-dimensional above ground sites and structures. Then I discovered the Tantur Scripture Gardens, where the past had been studiously re-created. Finding this theme garden answered my prayers! I stepped off the bus into a first-century tableau. Biblical plants and olive trees blossomed; signposts pointed to a sheepfold, a stone altar, and a garden tomb. To complete this drama, a Scandinavian television crew, with a cast of costumed Israelis, was filming action at the winepress. Yes, barefoot peasants actually stomped out grapes, with red juice flowing along troughs in the stone floor. The juice was ladled into large clay jars with gauze covers that strained out the flies. What authenticity! I took photos and made sketches that later became finished pen-and-ink drawings.

Thanks to God, these pictures now appear in Bibles to give visualization and meaning to verses such as Matthew 21:33: "He [Jesus] then began to speak to them in parables: A man planted a vineyard. He put a wall around it, dug a pit for the winepress and built a watchtower."

Some images I could only research in books, and so I traveled on foot to the exclusive library in the Palestinian quarter of the old city. Arab vendors selling brightly dyed purple, red, and orange scarves and trinkets bargained in rapid-fire Arabic inside a narrow alleyway connecting the old city to the Damascus Gate. I squeezed through the crushing crowd while tightly gripping my precious photo ID card that allowed me to enter Jerusalem's oldest and largest theological library, *The Ecole Biblique.*

I found a heavily locked entrance gate and felt a moment of distress. But then I noticed the intercom imbedded in the thick stone wall. Whew! I identified myself with the card, and the gates opened. History met me at the door with the scent of antique paper and well-worn leather bindings. Suddenly, I felt somehow out of place. Feeling theologically inferior, academically unqualified, and somewhat overwhelmed, I asked myself what I was doing here. To be engaged in study at this large and prestigious library was an emotional moment to cherish. But reality returned, and I began my research on ancient chariots—only to discover the computerized catalog was in French! I needed a French-English dictionary. I found one, and began entering words into the computer. There was much helpful information there, and I knew I would be returning for more.

On my last visit to the library, I got into an embarrassing situation. The tomblike library was positively airless. All the antique windows were tightly shut. Finding the stuffy atmosphere almost unbearable and thinking the other "bookworms" found it stuffy, too, I boldly swung wide-open a nearby window, leaned out, and deeply inhaled the wonderful fresh air. Suddenly, one of the "men in black" broke the library silence by shouting words like "Idiot!" and "Stupid!" I jerked my head inside only to see him glaring directly at me! In a heavy accent, he sternly told me "These books are treasures, and they must not be exposed to outside air," and he pulled the window shut with a bang! Humiliated, I gathered my papers, exited the stuffy library, and went to the nearby steps of St. Stephen's church to lick my wounds. Sitting on the ancient steps, I prayed, "Oh, God, forgive me as I try to live up to the expectations and culture of my hosts."

Having the information on ancient chariots in hand, I reviewed my research assignment list. Next were animals, birds, and reptiles. I had heard about a place where snakes were kept and I headed out with my sketchbook and pencils. The Israeli bus driver slowed down, signaling my destination; I climbed out onto the sidewalk near the Jerusalem Reptile Zoo across the street from the President's Mansion. *A strange place to harbor poisonous snakes*, I thought. *What if a missile hit the zoo and released the deadly creatures into the neighborhood?*

Behind a high wire fence, temporary wooden buildings stood in a dusty landscape. I approached what looked like an office, where a Jewish man dressed in faded blue work clothes sat tilting precariously on an old chair. Wondering whether he understood English, I enunciated, "I want to draw a picture of a viper." Incredulous and thinking he had misunderstood me, the man asked me in broken English to repeat my words. My sketchbook helped as I showed him a page of animal sketches and explained my presence. He abruptly rose, turned, and motioned for me to follow him.

Where is he taking me? I wondered. He led me through a wood-framed building into a small room with floor-to-ceiling shelves. I guessed this to be the inner sanctum of aquarium-like cages enclosing the most dangerous serpents. The keeper chose a cage and lifted it down. The top screened lid was locked, but I shivered with fear. What had I gotten myself into?

He led me outside, and I obediently followed him. We stopped at a low tree stump, where he gently placed the cage with its soon-to-be still-life model. Then he reached into his pocket, pulled out a key, and unlocked the lid. So far, so good—until he reached into the cage.

That was too much! *Was he going to bring the viper out for me to draw?* I wasn't about to stay. But, no, he just moved a rock concealing the drowsy reptile so I could get a better view.

My fingers raced to break my sketching record of one minute. The snake lay still, not rippling a muscle, and I relaxed as I drew the geometric ochre and brown scaly pattern. When I got to the snake's eye, it winked at me, and I knew everything was OK. Finished, I motioned for the guard to fetch his viper. He grinned widely when shown the drawing of his familiar snake friend.

Not knowing exactly which subjects I would be illustrating, I sketched many things: live animals at the zoo, mounted animals and birds in the Natural History Museum, olive and pomegranate trees, flowers, plants, and people. I discovered the Temple Institute, where Jews are anticipating the rebuilding of the Jerusalem Temple and have researched and constructed more than 90 sacred temple vessels and priestly garments. The docent allowed me to sketch and photograph some of these accurate replicas of the original temple furnishings. The Temple Institute was a treasure trove!

Eventually, I also visited the archeological museum with my camera. I blithely snapped pictures of a few valuable ancient objects until another one of those "men in black" with a booming voice informed me that I was breaking the rules. Again, I apologized and, red-faced once more, dropped the camera into my bag and switched to my "kosher" sketchbook before they could expel me.

As a Bible illustrator, I often wondered how I could capture spiritual truth in visual form. For me, God's radiance glowed in Jerusalem's white limestone buildings. God's glory colored the breathtaking cloudless sunsets of the Holy Land. I imagined them as airbrushed.

His power created the many scenic rock formations that I beheld. All around me during my visit were subjects worthy of recording and remembering for his purposes.

Some impressions of this Holy Land were known only by my spirit. My awareness was not illumined with the presence of long-dead saints and prophets of old but with an immediate sense of God—here and now. I felt the love of God for his beloved city. I experienced his presence in many places. I realized why so many Jews, Muslims, and Christians all claim Jerusalem as their city, their home, their heart's place. As I pondered and prayed about all my experiences in this sacred land, the Holy Spirit within me answered all my questions in time. He provided the means for me to be in Israel; he enabled me to sketch subjects that would become 200 pen-and-ink Bible illustrations, to be used in hundreds of languages around the world. Through the Holy Spirit, he is available to empower anyone of us.

Leaving Israel, the land of my Lord Jesus, caused surprising heartache. On the airport bus, I met a Jewish American man who asked me whether I enjoyed my visit, and he went on to tell me he had returned to Israel 34 times and looked forward to coming back again. It seemed implausible at first, yet now I could understand his love for his homeland, and I joined him in his desire to return, because Israel, in a spiritual sense, became my "homeland," too.

Inside the Ben Gurion air terminal, I frantically checked my pockets and purse for my ticket and passport. They were missing! After moments of apprehension and confusion, I heard a loudspeaker call out, "Will Louise Bass please come to the ticket-counter immediately!" Gratefully, I responded and was chided by an irate agent waving my papers and shouting, "Never, EVER lay down your travel documents in the ladies' room, madam!"

It was time to leave this inspiring land with my vivid memories, new friendships, important knowledge, valuable photos and sketches, and a desire to invest all of this into Bible illustrations for the benefit of others.

12

JOY-FILLED LIFE

Returning home to Michigan from Israel with my numerous sketches, photos, and slides, I hoped my precious portfolio contained everything I needed for the work ahead. My many sensations, spiritual experiences, and inspirations from the Holy Land could never be lost, as my passport and ticket had been, but since life is full of activities and distractions, I feared I might forget. Could my memories of all the classes I attended, the customs I observed, and the culture I participated in fail me? Limited as I was by my human brain—would I forget those necessary details?

I found comfort and reassurance in several places. First, I remembered a Bible verse in John's Gospel, chapter 14, verse 2: "But the Counselor, the Holy Spirit, whom the Father will send in my name, will teach you all things and will remind you of everything I have said to you."

Second, in her book *The Helper*, author Catherine Marshall addressed the problem of forgetfulness. She wrote:

> *"My exciting discovery was that Jesus' promise is much more inclusive than we have thought or dreamed. Once started on my walk in the Spirit, I found that the Helper had quietly become the living repository of my mind—that intricate human brain that still baffles scientists—the Chief Librarian of my lifetime's storehouse of memory, thoughts, quotations, and all kinds of specific data. He was now in charge of the whole, and I could trust Him to locate and retrieve out of the voluminous stacks of memory whatever I needed."*

What a comfort! What a relief! What a gift! Encouraged by Jesus' words, I, too, joined Mrs. Peter Marshall in her discovery—the Holy Spirit is the Chief Librarian. I embraced his assistance. He often sharpened my mind to details that were dull or slipping away in the rush of the complexities of life. In fact, I think I must have been one of his library's most frequent patrons!

Before many days at home, a packet of instructions from the United Bible Society arrived. Several alterations to the Horace Knolls illustrations required some work first and then I could begin the mind-boggling commission of creating nearly 200 pen-and-ink illustrations. Not only did the bible society send lists of animate and inanimate objects to be included in my drawings but also they requested several dramatic scenes featuring crowds of biblical characters to be incorporated.

Drawing Jesus speaking from a boat to hundreds of listeners on the shore posed a challenge. Thankfully, because of my early fashion-drawing training, drawing figures in ancient attire would be possible. But I did require models. I began my search among my church friends. I would have preferred male models with naturally dark hair and beards like the Eastern peoples I needed to draw. However, they were a minority among the blond, blue-eyed congregation of my church. So, I chose those who were willing to pose and I added the dark hair and beards as needed to the drawings.

The next step in this venture was creating and sewing several basic unisex robes for authenticity. On a sunny day in my backyard, a group of young adult men gathered to assist me in this unique task. Somewhat sheepishly, they donned robes and sandals and posed for my camera, bowing, kneeling, conversing, and overturning the temple tables. I wondered what thoughts were going through the minds of my neighbors and passersby when they saw four men in ancient robes, forming a chorus line and breaking into song!

After many months of praying and pouring myself into creating believable ink renderings, I completed the commission. It gave me immense satisfaction, but the job was not finished. The next step required meeting in Dallas with a group of Bible Society experts and Wycliffe translation scholars to check out the illustrations. As a relatively unknown artist, I wondered whether their questions and evaluations of my drawings might tempt me to be defensive. In the sky between Michigan and Texas, I prayed to calm my fears, and this verse came to my memory.

"When you are brought before the synagogues, rulers and authorities do not worry how you will defend yourselves or what you will say, for the Holy Spirit will teach you at that time what you should say" Luke 12:11.

Even though these Christian mission executives were not "rulers," they were highly dedicated to biblical accuracy. Not only must the text be authentic but also the illustrations must be factual—true to the original article. I knew I had done my very best.

Upon arriving in the large, well-lit meeting room in Dallas, I saw the panel of Bible experts seated behind a long, narrow table. The men greeted me, and one said, "Please take a seat, Mrs. Bass." I settled into a chair across from the table. One by one, the drawings were scrutinized by each individual without comment and then passed on quietly to the next person on the panel.

Say something! I cried out in my mind. *Say anything—ANYTHING!*

Finally, one of the men questioned the dimensions of a sacrificial altar, and I explained to him that I had examined several researched reproductions of altars in Israel and I had measured them. I could confidently vouch for the dimensions. This answer gave them reason to consider my credentials, earlier overlooked. When they became more aware of my qualifications, which included knowledge of cultural dress and furnishings, accuracy of biblical representation, and careful research, we all relaxed.

However, the panel did discover a cultural error in one of my drawings. The picture depicted the following Bible scene:

"The crowd joined in the attack against Paul and Silas, and the magistrates ordered them to be stripped and beaten. After they had been severely flogged, they were thrown into prison and the jailor was commanded to guard them carefully. Upon receiving such orders, he put them in the inner cell and fastened their feet in the stocks." Acts 16:22-24.

I had visualized this scene with Paul's and Silas's feet locked in stocks similar to those observed in colonial America, with their barefoot soles facing the viewer. Not knowing but quickly learning, I discovered that portraying the soles of one's feet was an obscenity in Jewish culture at that time. It would require redrawing the men to present a side view. Other than that one easily corrected cultural error, the Dallas group gave me the "green light" to finalize the illustrations. Relieved and encouraged, I silently offered a prayer of thanks to Almighty God. I gathered my precious portfolio, caught a cab to the airport, and flew home to Michigan.

Later in my studio, I redrew the prison scene and mailed it to the bible society. They readily approved and accepted the revised version of the illustration. God graciously provided for me once again and allowed my gift of creativity to be used in his Kingdom work. How faithful is his care!

The 200 Bible illustrations were published in catalogs by the United Bible Society and Wycliffe Bible Translators. Earlier illustrators such as Horace Knowles, an Englishman, and Annie Vallotton, a Norwegian woman, also illustrated many Bibles. Translators in various countries who are ready to have their Old or New Testaments printed have access to all of these illustrations. I am overjoyed and always feel a glow when I hear about a newly printed Bible containing some of my drawings. Illustrations are capable of moving readers to greater understanding of the text because the spiritual truth is in visual, as well as written, form.

On one occasion while I was standing with friends in the foyer of an old ivy-covered gray stone church in North Carolina, a man behind me gently tapped my shoulder and said, "I'm a Bible translator from Peru, South America, and we use your artwork in our Bibles to help the readers understand the words and the culture." It made the work worthwhile.

Another time, a missionary to Thailand sent me a copy of the Northern Khmer New Testament that used some of my illustrations.

I certainly couldn't read the language, but I hoped the Northern Khmer people who could read it found some of the stories more meaningful because of the drawings. One of them was the drawing of Paul and Silas in prison. I had no idea of the stretch of God's arm in using these pictures.

About the time I finished the illustrations and sent them off, my church handed out booklets seeking volunteers to work in other cultures and countries. I wondered whether there were any overseas opportunities for graphic artists. I searched the listings and came across one that read, "Artist needed to travel to the state of Chiapas in southern Mexico to design eye-catching Bible-based posters in the Tzeltal Indian language." I considered whether this might be God providing me another well-timed chance to "stretch the tent curtains wide." Ever since I opened my life to the work of the Holy Spirit, he had enabled me to fulfill others' needs that were met by my God-given creative gifts of drawing and painting.

I contacted my church headquarters in Grand Rapids, Michigan, and learned that the posters would take several weeks to complete. Then they would be placed in local Tzeltal-speaking Christian churches for their pastors to display as visual aids clarifying Bible passages for children and adults. I learned about the approximately 190,000 speakers of the Tzeltal language, mostly living in the state of Chiapas, Mexico. These are direct descendants of the ancient Mayan Indian people. I decided my answer would be "Yes, I'll go!" I believed the Holy Spirit chose me to take this far-away opportunity to help these people understand their Tzeltal Bibles.

Chiapas, Mexico, brought back memories of long ago. Jack and I, with baby Jonathan, lived there in "jungle camp" and learned jungle survival skills when we first became missionaries. This time I stayed not far from that old camp, in Buenos Aires, a small mission center and Bible school overseen by Reformed Church missionaries. A volunteer typist traveled with me. She and I stayed in a modest apartment and ate with the friendly mission people in their homes. In addition to our assignments of typing and illustrating, we went sightseeing and visited nearby villages. We attended overflowing, enthusiastic Bible-believing churches built from local sun-dried bricks and palm fronds. Colorful hand-woven clothing, rhythmic Latin music, and picturesque villages composed a backdrop to the stage of inspiration.

One of my challenges turned out to be accurately portraying the peoples' facial features. The Tzeltal people of Mayan Indian descent have a unique cheekbone structure and hairline. I enjoyed sketching these appealing and friendly folks. Visual application of biblical truth in a language unknown to me brought gratification, and the posters were finished almost too quickly. I returned to the United States with a renewed and refreshed outlook and a strong desire to continue to use my God-given gifts for his glory.

13

PAINTING WITH
PURPOSE

After a happy reunion with friends and family in Michigan and "ooing" and "aahing" at the accomplishments of my grandchildren, it felt good to be home again. Still, I occasionally wondered where my Guide might take me next. Each of my artwork tasks had a story of its own: Papua New Guinea literacy books, Kenyan reading charts, Israeli research materials, 200 Bible illustrations, and Mexican teaching posters.

I came to a lull. I wasn't painting, at least not much. My creativity had reached a standstill—perhaps a fallow time. I thought about pictures I had painted in the past. Then I received an unexpected reminder.

I was sitting in my church pew one Sunday morning, and a senior couple sat down near me. When the friendship folder passed to the woman, she saw my name, leaned toward me, and asked, "Did you paint a picture for my daughter about 20 years ago?"

Yes, I recollected the scene of two innocent young boys walking near a dangerous precipice with an angel behind them. The boys' parents had loaned me photos of their sons and asked me to produce an oil painting to represent God watching over them, protecting them from harm. Now their grandmother was telling me how the portrait made an impact on the boys' lives and was still cherished by the family. The painting hangs in the grandparents' home as a reminder to pray for their grandsons. These boys are married men now. They confess Jesus Christ as their Lord and Savior, and they worship in Christian churches in the state where they reside.

I received a blessing as I thought about how God, in his grace, had indeed used me, an ordinary individual who desired to be everything he created me to be. He called, employed, motivated, and enabled me to do so.

Once, I wished I could paint a portrait of the Holy Spirit. It would need to be impressionistic, of course. My search through the Old Masters brought up hundreds of representations of Jesus mirroring the artists' culture and time period. A search for pictures of God the Father produced paintings such as Michelangelo's magnificent painting on the Sistine Chapel ceiling with God's hand reaching out to create man.

A search for representations of the Holy Spirit turned up white doves and red flames. Was there another way I could translate invisible truth into visual reality? Since I could not see this powerful force, I would depend on biblical occurrences and my own experience to represent God's Spirit.

He existed from eternity, before the beginning of time. I knew from the book of Genesis that when God created heaven and earth, "The Spirit of God was hovering over the waters." In the New Testament book of Acts, Jesus told his disciples to wait and they would be baptized with the Holy Spirit and they would receive power and spiritual gifts.

What about others called to serve God with their artistic ability? What about other creative activities happening in poetry, music, teaching, preaching, writing, drama, and more? I greatly needed to be inspired and motivated by creative colleagues. My search ended when I learned of an organization called Christians in the Visual Arts (CIVA). I drove to Calvin College in Grand Rapids, where members got together for lively meetings. Creative speakers put ideas into words inspiring our hearts and our work. An upcoming Christian art show was announced, and I knew I would enter the show with a new canvas depicting God's Spirit.

The resulting oil painting became a visual impression of the words of the prophet Ezekiel, chapter 47. It paralleled my journey. Water from the Temple of God flowed into a river while someone walked ever deeper into it, in four stages. "Water up to the ankles" symbolized the initial work of God's Spirit in a person's life. "Water up to the knees" represented growth and prayer in the spiritual life. "Water up to the waist" implied possible difficulties but determination to continue. "Water to swim in" represented our trust as we are buoyed up in a cleansing baptism. As Ezekiel refers to the increasing depth of the measured water, in like manner, our Christian life becomes deeper, richer, as we thrive on the living water of Jesus' words.[1]

I submitted my new painting to the exhibit, hoping yet doubting it would be accepted. To my surprise, on my arrival at the show, I saw my painting in the center of a large gallery hung with many colorful canvases. A blue ribbon award adorned its frame. This unusual painting attracted an assortment of viewers; some people offered me their various interpretations of its meaning. Momentarily, I thought the assortment of insights meant flaws in my work—missing the mark of my purpose. Then, graciously, the Holy Spirit reminded me that he is the preparer of hearts and minds and it is his timing and not mine that determines the revelation of God's message to hearts through visual art. No two observers of a piece of art will perceive it in exactly the same way.

Consequently, I began to consider another painting, one that would interpret the Trinity without the third person, mirroring my past life without him. Where to start? In Papua New Guinea, I sometimes experienced physical weakness, sadness, and fear. My understanding of the Holy Trinity had included God our Heavenly Father; Jesus, our Savior; and an unknown entity called the Holy Spirit. How could I portray that concept in a visual piece? What symbols could I use?

Those thoughts popped up as I walked on a nearby trail where bikers sometimes camped. Strolling along, I suddenly noticed a piece of dull metal pipe abandoned in the overgrown grass. It looked about two feet long, with a crosspiece at one end topped by three faucets.

---

[1] I am indebted to the late Dr. Alan Redpath of Moody Bible Institute for his interpretation of the words of Ezekiel. This was the topic of a teaching given at a pre-Easter conference in New Guinea. I do not know whether Dr. Redpath ever wrote or published this interpretation in any of his many books.

The disconnected pipe gave me an idea. That piece of discarded plumbing became my inspiration!

I began to visualize the open left-hand faucet as a symbol of God the Creator represented by gushing water cascading down, creating lush vegetation to spring up from the earth beneath. The open central faucet symbolized Jesus Christ, with water flowing and creating a River of Life. The third faucet, also capable of a mighty outpouring, would be turned off above a barren landscape, representing the result of shutting out the work of the Holy Spirit. The Holy Spirit waits for our invitation to turn on the glorious power source.

Eagerly, I planned and prepared a palette of paints for the painting. Unfortunately, it never got put to use. I had an accident! I slipped on an icy street, and my right wrist was fractured; the cast and sling made painting impossible. Fine brushwork was out of the question, but I could grasp a lightweight square of artist's black graphite in my hand. In spite of my handicap, the picture of the water faucets slowly emerged at my drawing board. When completed, I hung this drawing of a cross-shaped pipe with three faucets, two with water flowing and one without, in my studio as a reminder of my empty past.

How do I know God loves our creativity and desire for beauty? At the very beginning of the Bible, in Genesis 1:2, it is written that "the earth was formless and empty, darkness was over the surface of the deep, and the Spirit of God was hovering over the waters." He played an essential part in the creation of the world.

The second time we read about the Spirit of God is in Exodus, when Moses announced,

> *"See, the Lord has chosen Bezalel son of Uri, the son of Hur, of the tribe of Judah, and he has filled him with the Spirit of God, with skill, ability and knowledge in all kinds of crafts—to make artistic designs for work in gold silver and bronze, to cut and set stones, to work in wood and to engage in all kinds of artistic craftsmanship."*
> — EXODUS 30:33

Wow! Just think of the recognition and importance God gives to creativity.

This same Holy Spirit, who worked at the beginning of time and creation and later empowered Bezalel to create a tabernacle, is available to us today. When we receive God's gift of salvation by accepting Jesus Christ as our Savior, we avail ourselves of many blessings. We receive

forgiveness of our sins. We are new creations in Christ and are given spiritual gifts. When we offer God beauty in our poetry, music, care giving, painting, teaching, administering, etc, our works will glorify him. The fabulous benefit of being employed by the Holy Spirit is that our work is a delight. We need to probe the deepest recesses of our hearts and ask God to reveal our spiritual gifts to use in his service for others.

"Follow the way of love and eagerly desire spiritual gifts."
— 1 CORINTHIANS 14:1

His possibilities are exciting and never ending!

afterword

Driving alone in my old green Buick in 2010, I was on my way to visit cousins in Ontario. My mind shifted into neutral. Suddenly, I heard a clear voice in my head, slowly saying, "I want you to write a book." *Oh, no—not me! I can't!* Once, I tried to write a book, but the rejection slips suggested I might try something else.

Rarely had I heard God's voice, but this was unmistakable. After grasping the source of the words and wiping tears from my cheeks, I decided to test this communication and let God know he had the wrong person. If he did want me to write anything, I would require the following: a spirit-filled editor, a spacious and solitary workplace, and a Christian writer's workshop to attend.

Within weeks, at the Maranatha Christian Writers' Conference, I met my indispensable editor, Ann Wilkinson. I was offered workspace in Virginia Walsh's spacious home near Lake Michigan. God met all my needs and excuses. Friend Fred Hofstra guided me through the computer's bewildering secrets. Others, including Tom Johnson, Aretta Loving, and Bob and Edna Shoobridge, helped with reading, suggestions, and encouragement.

With the end of the manuscript coming into view, I began to pray for a publisher. From a friend, I unexpectedly received a gift that enabled me to utilize the services of Jenkins Group, whose motto is "to help aspiring authors get good work out there." With their professional helping hands, they made this book a reality.

I experienced joy but also struggled with heartfelt grief during the book's creation. On January 15, 2012, Jonathan, our firstborn child, was called home by the Lord at the age of 52. He had gone to New Guinea with us when he was two and then returned to America for his education, marriage, and family life. He suffered from a very painful and incurable hereditary skin disease.

I and my family and our friends received comfort from our Heavenly Father as he ministered consolation through his people. Classmates from Papua New Guinea school days wrote uplifting letters, poems, and e-mails expressing their love and prayers during Jonathan's long time of suffering. Caring people baked cookies and brought casseroles and tasty soups for our family and visitors. At Jonathan's funeral, his pastor, Rick, brought solace and hope, and Rick's son blessed us with the gift of his voice as he sang a song by Bart Millard, "I Can Only Imagine." A young Sunday school student of Jonathan's wrote him a note and slipped it into his open casket. Much love was evident at his service. Many people extended loving sympathy to us along with their tributes to Jonathan's integrity, faithfulness, and sense of humor.

When we as Christians love and obey God the Father, Jesus the Son, and the Holy Spirit, we are empowered and given hope to cope with difficulties, grief, and loss knowing we are in his hands.

> *"May the God of hope fill you with all joy and peace as you trust in him, so that you may overflow with hope by the power of the Holy Spirit."*
> — *ROMANS 15:13*

ABOUT THE AUTHOR

LOUISE BASS was born in Detroit and accepted Jesus' call on her life when she was a teenager. She trained in fashion illustration and worked in an art studio until she met and married her husband, Jack. They studied linguistics and were accepted into the Wycliffe Bible Translators mission. For 20 years, they worked in Papua New Guinea. Louise illustrated reading primers, while Jack assisted translators to assure accuracy. After Jack's death at 51, she raised their three children. Later, she did artwork in Kenya, Mexico, and Israel, where she created 200 black and white Bible illustrations that are used in Bibles worldwide today.

To contact Louise or to order additional copies of this book,
please email basspondbook@gmail.com.